· *Breakers* ·

·*Breakers*·

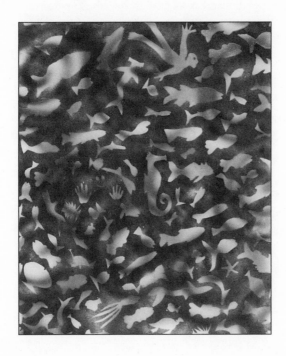

SELECTED POEMS BY PAUL VIOLI

COFFEE HOUSE PRESS

Coffee House Press is an independent nonprofit literary publisher supported in part by a grant provided by the Minnesota State Arts Board, through an appropriation by the Minnesota State Legislature, and in part by a grant from the National Endowment for the Arts. Significant support has also been provided by the McKnight Foundation; the Star Tribune Foundation; the Lila Wallace-Reader's Digest Fund; the Bush Foundation; the Target Foundation; General Mills Foundation; St. Paul Companies; Honeywell Foundation; Patrick and Aimee Butler Family Foundation; the law firm of Schwegman, Lundberg, Woessner & Kluth, P.A.; and many individual donors. To you and our many readers across the country, we send our thanks for your continuing support.

Coffee House Press books are available to the trade through our primary distributor, Consortium Book Sales & Distribution, 1045 Westgate Drive, Saint Paul, MN 55114. For personal orders, catalogs, or other information, write to: Coffee House Press, 27 North Fourth Street, Suite 400, Minneapolis, MN 55401.

www.coffeehousepress.org

COVER ART Dale Devereux Barker
COVER + BOOK DESIGN Kelly N. Kofron
AUTHOR PHOTOGRAPH David S. Kelley

Library of Congress Cataloging-in-Publication Data

Violi, Paul, 1944 –
    Breakers : selected poems/ by Paul Violi.
    p. cm.
    ISBN 1-56689-099-3 (alk. paper)
    I. Title.

PS35782.I59 A6 2000
811'.54—dc21

00-022776

10   9   8   7   6   5   4   3   2   1

Printed in Canada

for
Helen & Alex

Contents

Acknowledgments

The author wishes to express his gratitude to the publishers of the books in which these poems previously appeared, and especially to Bill Zavatsky and Bob Hershon.

"Harmatan," from *Harmatan,* Sun Press, NY, 1977.

"Triptych," from *Splurge,* Sun Press, NY, 1981.

"King Nasty" and "Little Testament," from *Likewise,* Hanging Loose Press, NY, 1988.

"Wet Bread and Roasted Pearls" and "The Curious Builder," from *The Curious Builder,* Hanging Loose Press, NY, 1993.

"The Hazards of Imagery" selections are from *Fracas,* Hanging Loose Press, NY, 1998. An earlier version of this poem formed the text of a collaboration done with printmaker Dale Devereux Barker.

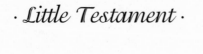

· *Little Testament* ·

Little Testament

To wake on my fortieth birthday
buried in this pile of gifts
and not question how they
or I got here
but proceed with the inventory,
all tatters and extra coda,
and salvage for you what I can
from whatever is fake and forgettable:

Something old, something new, something
borrowed, stolen, scavenged,
a lot simply looted
from the pleasures and shambles of the day.

Tobacco, wine, sacks of cash,
a menagerie, a matador's doormat
and a little bull,
The Sultan of Passion's Manual,
a semi-epithalamion,
Sonata for Brutality and Vegetable,
snapshots, a winged thing,
what looks like a self-portrait
of Ponce de Leon's younger brother, Pounce.

Pick or choose,
keep or toss.
Welcome to a firesale at the local Cornucopia.
Please excuse the whiff of chaos.

Forty years old
and I still can't see myself

planting flowers
on either the dark edge of heaven or hell.

Though in either place
I can guess which would flourish,
I have a better idea
of what thrives here.
Item: And so, instead of a bribe
for my gravekeeper,
I leave a trillium,

a lovely plant
that smells like rotten meat,
or any other flowering contradiction
whose colors attract bees
but whose stench draws flies;
whose pollination depends
on an insult as well as beauty.

And I guess you can get to Limbo
the same way you got here:
by mistake.
And I like to think
you can still get to heaven
with the right disguise.
But in either place
I'd be disappointed
if monotony were more than a buzz.
I hope to hear
a frequent hum of satisfaction,
or inspiration,
the little wings of an immensity,
a thought in god's mind.

But I'll settle for a bumblebee.
According to the known laws
of propriety and aerodynamics
it shouldn't get off the ground
but does, half wonder and
—by sheer force of will—half ridiculous.

Bees, after all, got me started on this,
their loose formality.
I had seen a lump of gold in the road,
and looking closer realized
it was a pile of them, bees
who like ferocious translators
had taken on the shape
of what they were devouring: a dead frog.
And I thought: François Villon,
Form Giver! Merci beaucoup!

Item: Ah, dear Formalists,
how you persevere.
You whose sleek instinct
for the unanswerable
has been thwarted, whose wish to fly
has left you often unable to crawl,
whose high romance slithers in lines
like a fuse of clarity,
like a slow trickle over chrome,
only to quietly go down the drain,
please accept my gratitude in the form of
The Snake's Fable:

How an anaconda becomes
trapped by what it seeks.

How it squirms through a fence
and swallows the egret
that was left as bait.
How it then fails to escape
through the narrow fenceposts.
How its length becomes more distorted
—the shape of the bird, the form
within the form, as if it had caught
its own soul
and choked on it.

You can have your snake and egret too.

Item: Now for you, my several friends,
in honor of your trust,
your warmth, your jokes:
Champagne . . . in a dirty glass.
Though not just any glass:
the finest old Venetian,
so light and clear you would think
the Air herself
had placed her hand in yours

and a cool secret on your lips.
How light touches its delicate rim,
curves into serenity with a smirk,
the glint that was in the eye
of its maker, the Venetian
who tried to get glass this thin
believing that it would shatter
if ever a drop of poison
were added to the wine.

It was a doge-eat-doge world alright.

And not just any champagne.
A magnum, a Methuselah
of The Blushful Hippocrene.
In the Cellars of the Pearly Dark,
a rack reserved for each of you.

You can sip it like a wolf,
you can lap it like a dog,
guzzle it like a Vandal,
swig it like a saint.
You can take the bottles
(Why do they, like hearts,
always seem heavier when empty?)
and toss them through the skylight.
Hell's bells . . .

Or any goon's chance
to scatter the angels
who from their withering heights
leer down
through the glare of everything
to see you embrace
under your bedsheet,
your sail of unconcern,
as it luffs above you
and every broken thing you own.

Item: Or keep the bottle,
for this Famous Ship in a Bottle Kit,
a replica
of the Sultan of Passion's Flagship.

Built to reign over a great lake
that almost dried up

before she was launched
—and afterward,
as everyone expected,
did just that—the majestic ship
plowed through the crud-laden waters
and ever-encroaching shoreline
like an agitated duck
that keeps a last puddle clear
on a freezing pond;

constantly on the move,
in ever-tighter circles,
all futility and quacking isolation,
while the squalid wordlings
in her crew
sang "Gimme Dat Ole Time Derision"
and the last of the lake
evaporated under the hull,
leaving their ship
as high and dry as a cathedral.

Item: Junior Visigoth, puerile drudge,
instead of standing forlorn
on a sultry pier
on a Sunday morn
fishing for rats,

take the job you were born for:
—Calvary to the rescue!—
Managing the Souvenir Concession
at St. Pat's.

Though behind
that tintinabular cash register,

you'll never lose sight
of your mascot.
High on a scavenger's vantage point,
the tallest tree on that hill,
the dead one without a branch,

perched like a black flame
on a candle,
illuminating nothing
—less than nothing—for miles around,
there he'll be, your ragged crow.

Item: And the few hawks
always ready to zero in
on any vital thing,
they belong to you, dear Cynic.

You get to stand further out
in the future,
so whenever another horde appears
grunting before the wide-open gates
of this new century,
you're the one who gets to tell them
they're too early.

The one to tell them
they are not the first to stare
into the cold beauty of indifference
without a god to defend them.

They'll look over your shoulder.
They'll want to see the womenfolk.
They'll ask if thoughts
will now enter their minds
like nudes in a fog.
They'll want to kiss an aerodrome.

But you will get to tell them
that no matter where they turn
—city, lake, plain—
the view will stop them
dumb in their tracks,
will spread right through them
as it does you,
so clear and strange
like a disappointing vision,

spread flat and low
across the lake
with such ease,
the urge to say anything
lies scattered out there
with the shadows of a breeze.

Their horses lick the frost
off the ground,
their banners droop,
they're finally lost.

They'll look into your face
and into a distance beyond winter,
beyond change,
further than any hunger
has ever led them.
And overhead, in the only bough
whose leaves have yet to fall

—leaves stiff, leaning in the last direction
the wind blew them—
your flag still flies.

Clockwise, the hawks slip away.

Item: And you, occasional poet,
I award you a ton of sympathy,
a place to dump it,
and this variation on a theme:
It's not the heat, it's the cupidity.

It's not the squalid kitchen,
the boiled chicken, the burnt sneaker,
the steam in a white sink.

It's not the four million tons
of cosmic dust
that gravity gathers
and drops on earth each day.
It's your own squandered magic,
the weight of your own quiet voice.
It's the peculiar sense of nothing
when the middle of nowhere shifts again.
It's the quiet, disappointing extreme,
another long-deserted drive-in movie
at high noon, titles

still dangling from the marquee
in busted poems, speaker wire
ripped from rusted pipe,
dry weeds in the gravel.
It's the endless intermission,
the stalled ocean,
the blank screen's faded lunar curve
tilted high over the asphalt's faded waves.

Item: And out of this,
occasional Nihilist,
there's no quick way for you,

but in the occasional detail, a general direction;
in the scuffed moss, an idle clue,
softness rooted in granite;
in the cool, quiet wood, a place
to think or hope; in birch leaves
and splayed branches
layered with shadows of leaves,
a kind of listening;

in mud and leaf mold, a deer track;
in the brush, a sapling
corkscrewed by a vine;
in jumbled stone, pieces
of an eventual flow;
in a cracked rock, a lucky streak;
in an old bone, an unexpected lightness;
in cloudbanks of lush green hills
fading into clouds, a world on the rise;

in a blackened, overgrown foundation,
a matter of fact;
in a scorched chimney, a new nest;
in fern and laurel, a hard twist
and a gentleness;

in the hemlock, in its lowest limb,
an easy reach or heavy wing's descent;
in its gently splintered shade,
a dark end in a kind and crystal eye;
in the well, in its clogged shaft,
a little song of loss (maybe yours, maybe not);
in the spiderweb that spans it,
anticipation's skeleton;
in the red spider
that makes it tremble,

a cunning gentleness, a quick heart,
maybe yours, maybe not.

Item: To my wife, Ann,
I leave this littered house
and all it contains:
the comfort, the disarray, the panic,
the splendid lamps
that shine through the oaks,
the windows high and wide,
and the constellation
that we've traced
in winter's long view of the stars.

Each place we've known, each point
a knot in The Great Net,
cast from childhood to Asia, across
the longitude and lassitude of our time;
this notion, that there is
no end to what we are,
that tangled, snagged, and drawn,

the routes of our coming and going
converge here, gathered in the lights
spread over these black hills
and clustered in the city's heights,
for us to haul it in,
full of whatever we've done,
wherever we've been.

Item: To my son, Alexander,
I bequeath with love and admiration
the Arc de Triomphe.
And here's why:

To commemorate
the golden attitude you displayed
in the first moments of your life,
the magnificent arc you made
when the doctor
held you aloft in the cold air
and you twisted and turned,
scattering everyone
in the delivery room
as you pissed all over us.

Item: To my daughter, Helen,
I leave a prime Elysian lot,
that island-meadow
you rode into
late one afternoon
and let your horse wade at will,
stir up wildflower
and milkweed
in the purpling blue,

so that the silver seed
hovered far around you,
made you smile
amid innumerable smiles
and raised in a casual swarm
years of waves and glinting wings.

Whatever favor, whatever truth
there was of Elysium
filled your eyes
and you laughed at the mystery of things
like one of god's spies
when the sun
coaxed your soul into sight

then drew your name
in the air, Loved-of-Light.
(Or perhaps you saw it all
in a less mawkish way:
the grinning spirits,
the exaltation of shoppers
as they enter The Celestial Mall.)

Item: Dead-eye Dick,
the jubilant realist, where did he go?
And the bouncers
at the Tempus Fugit Funeral Parlor,
who gave them the heave-ho?

Polly and Esther,
the scrawny Rip-snorter
and Capability Jones?
The Fearless Fucker, the Blizzard Dancer,
when the bottles slipped
out of their frozen gloves,
where did they go?
Where does the hasty music lead?
The happy rat-tracks in the snow?

What happened to Elmer
and Daffy, Big Bertha, and Limp Louie?
Bashful, Happy, and Grumpy?
Comatose, Ecstatic, and Berserk?
What are all these blanks
in the summer street?
Whatever happened to that guy
who used to catch bullets in his teeth?

To them, to anyone
humbled, stricken by the beauty

the world gives and takes,
here's the long and short of it:

In any of the blooming zeroes
one cloud sprinkles offshore,
in any crater on the moon,
lay down this life.

Item: Now, last readers,
I offer dypsomanic immunity
to any place you wish,
where all you need to do
is relax, stroll, hold hands
like absurdity and squalor,
and admire the indolent harbors
and unfinished memorials
to The Spirit of Laziness.

Where bridges and hours
span a mile or two more
than they did before,
confident splendors
suspended above the monstrous clamor,
the furious view
of another life below.

Where you don't have to spend
nights in a damp park
listening to swans fart in their sleep.
No more mornings that leave you
dizzy and stranded
on a pile of junk and generosity
or meandering
through zoos in rainlight,

the steamy cages,
the great apes whimpering in the mist,
the washed-out posters
announcing yet another concert
by Smug Paul and The Hedonists.

Now, for you, the tidal music
of evening resumes,
with its dockside antics and lunar revelry,
the private balcony
from which you can watch divers
as their flashlights
scan the harbor floor
for the pianos you've tossed to them.

Here's the chance
to catch up on sleep you lost long ago.
Find a loose hour or two
in a pile of rose leaves
steeped in sunlight and spilled wine,
in the kindlier motions
of silence and vagrant time

that may wake you on the move,
like the only birds in an early breeze,
like fish in a strong current,
like dirty spirits in starlight
—wake on the silver heels
of gods who vanish into their own jokes.

Item: Until then, forget all this clutter
but take this pearl.
It is the hard light, the soul
of the laziest thing that ever lived.

I didn't get around to—
I couldn't decide what to wrap it in,
which unfinished poem
or squandered conceit.
It would be easier
just to rip a page out of a book.
One that I remember describes
how in World War II
the writer Malaparte
while crossing the Lake Ladoga convoy route
during the siege of Leningrad
looked down through the ice
and saw innumerable human faces,
beautiful glass masks,
staring up at him.

Their lips thin and worn,
their hair long, their eyes large and clear
like delicate icons—the images of those
killed while attempting to cross
the only supply line to a ruined city.

Their bodies, submerged all winter,
had been swept away by the first spring currents,
but what remained, the expression their faces
had left etched in the ice,
he said it was serene
and that their eyes seemed to follow his
as he walked across the lake.

Or instead of that page,
I could use those stanzas by Arnaut Daniel
that Pound translated:

"Though all things freeze here,
    I can naught feel the cold,
For new love sees, here
    My heart's new leaf unfold;
So am I rolled
    And lapped against the breeze here:
Love, who doth mold
    My force, force guarantees here.

Aye, life's a high thing,
    Where joy's his maintenance,
Who cries 'tis a wry thing
    Hath danced never my dance.
I can advance
    No blame against fate's tithing
For lot and chance
    Have left the best thing my thing."

Or, instead of wrapping the pearl,
why don't I just roll it over to you,
ahead of the morning.
Let your eyes grow accustomed to it
as they did to the depths of the night,
and find how between your fingertips
it is a toy of thought.
Seed of obstinance, prize
of mood, sand and tide,
it is not the ball of light
that others wish the world to be
but what little sense
it can yield in a year and a day.
It is my own gift of darkness,
less than I mean, all I can say.

· *Harmatan* ·

Nigeria
December, 1966 – June, 1967

for Bill Zavatsky

I

Yesterday also has its leaves, newspapers
blown down the bare avenues
and streets of yet another city
entering the wide morning behind you, surprising
you that this light, often unnoticeable breeze
which constantly blows in your face,
which carries sights through your eyes
like leaves through air,
can move these cities farther away
than islands driven by an ocean stream
until all the buildings pale
and you can no longer hear the wooden bells,
the cats wailing in desolate markets,
nor the soft grinding sound
of waves large women made
scrubbing stone staircases
that spiraled up to a multitude of rooms.

2

You expected a certain kind of excitement
to cover the day,
waves rising to meet the rain,
but instead of rain
the sensation of an endless fall
rushes through your skin,
clocks slow down
screwing themselves into walls,
nothing remains of New York
but its light and then
a shadow drowns in darkness,
a sentient nightlong quietude
sunk in the surface of the air,
undisturbed except for one short breeze
that doesn't touch you
but rouses a few shapes in your mind,
figures groping for seats in a crowded theater,
faucets dripping in vast sinks . . .

The next morning, locust leaves
lodged as still as fossils in the humid sky.
An old brown woman sits
on a new aluminum staircase in Scarborough Station,
skirt folded back on her knees.
Spawning carp flop and swirl wearily
around the cove, ripples gliding
over to the willows, branches
hanging low, touching
their now moving reflections.

3

One place in the market selling meat.
The keeper waves a hand over the deck
of his stall and sends a blanket of flies aloft,
revealing a pile of diced lamb;
he rolls a handful in red pepper
and serves it in a sheet of newspaper.
A warm soda.
Lips numb from munching kola nuts.
In the glare of a Nigerian afternoon
your mind a grave for symbols.
An ancient woman sits in the dust.
Blind yellow eyes.
Two infants tug at her flattened breasts.
Storm clouds coming up behind her,
towering funnels of sand and straw
spinning across the fields. The driver yells,
wincing faces crowd into the back of the lorry.
Tin leaves rattling.
The woman stays under the creaking tree,
hoists a white robe over herself and the children,
dark cloud closing
like the lid of a shell over Kazaure Junction.

4

Harmatan: month-long winds off the Sahara.
Tents taut, straining.
In the morning, the sky's brown.
Step outside and vultures scatter
from the pots and bowls,
except one that drags himself away, ragged
feathers hanging in a singed cape
scraping the loose soil behind him.
Edges worn off old mud houses.
Mice have eaten the corners off a book:
a round copy of Hazlitt's criticism.
Warped rulers, clocks clogged with sand.
To discourage thieves, the wall
circling the compound frosted with broken bottles
buried neck-down along its mud crown
and now smoothed as glass found on a beach.
One at a time, at twilight, the vultures return,
swooping onto this leafless white tree
until there are so many
you can't see the branches.

5

Kaduna's tin roofs glinting in the afternoon.
Peanut sacks piled into hundred-foot pyramids.
Groups of lepers and beggars
converging on customers outside of stores.
Streets thick with exhaust fumes.
Khandee's heavy breasts.
Cock-eyed and slim-hipped. Flowery skirt.
Keeping mosquitoes off you all night.
Sweet, stoned, perpetually drowsy.
Black leg next to a white leg in candlelight.
Tongue leading a cool breeze over your skin.
Influenced by bad English movies,
she'd say: Dahling, Dahling
and, once in a while, request a few shillings
for another candle.
Come back after a month or two
of completing maps in the bush,
find a letter from P.J.
saying Khandee's in Kai-an-ji
where the Italians are building a dam
so there's plenty of food and money,
all the girls are there
boasting of white babies in their bellies.

6

Bees squirming on the desk
one night, staggering around the lantern
as if drunk with its light;
curled up as if stung by its light.
The bedroll kept open on a table
high off the floor in the center of the room.
One scorpion killed an hour before
just as it was about to puncture a big toe.
Maps and aerial photos of the Faskari area
rolled in a tin cylinder.
Mosquito net draped over the bedding,
tiny footballs of bat guano
sprinkled across the top.
After you turned the lantern off, the mantle
glowing redder than the scorpion,
fading with you into the dark
when you close your eyes.
The bats already frolicking overhead.
Fluttering circles.
You wait for the view,
for sleep to recede down oceanic slopes
baring a future, a few
of its enormous, unutterable details.

7

Beyond the sparkling glass embedded in the walls
a view of the heat, a colorless fire
shimmering waist-deep above the ground,
distorting huts, shifting fences.
Rocks floating in pools of air,
trees stretched as though they've not
gotten enough sun, the surface
of the red road split into planes
stirred by broad waves running beneath
as light spread before a sunset
swells with the rise and fall of the sea.
The cow still beside the road
where it fell a week ago,
hit by a truck, legs straight up,
vultures tugging at its eyes and tongue.
The dogs began to work on it
by the next day, eating through the asshole
until they could walk upright into the carcass;
every day the hide becoming more slack,
bees spilling out the eyes,
skin drooping against the rib cage
like a tent with loosened pegs and guys.

8

Delirium. Dengue. Your mind tries
to escape its teeming shadow.
Sights lit by black lightning.
At daybreak, drained by the shivering
that shook you off the bed,
wander out into the fields,
not sure where the limits are,
where a life begins or ends.
Fields burned a week or two ago;
the villagers burn them before planting.
Wildflowers already sprouting
yellow, star-like in the black grass;
refuge in their scented light.
Have a cigarette,
welcome yourself back.
Strike a match,
hand shaky with a strange gentleness.
One star in the sky and an imagined one,
faltering, letting go of its own brightness.

9

The sun passes over like a file,
sand trickles down the slopes.
Baobabs filled with the hum of unseen bees.
Branches ripped off, tied in bundles
and carried back to the huts for fuel.
Mango trees nodding, people asleep,
left out in the sun by the shifting shade.
Small boats beached by the sunken river.
Kneeling in its white bed, a group of women
scoop holes, strain water from the sand
and walk back singing; tall
and wrapped in night-blue robes,
clay jugs on their heads,
tribal scars on their faces: three lines
across one cheek, another down
the middle of the nose.
Soil dried out, sprayed in the wind.
Children blowing magic off a moth's wings.
Ground sunk to its desert skeleton.
The churning air above a patch of grass,
rife with gnats, slows down a bit;
a confusion you can't help but breathe.
You don't feel any larger
but everything else seems smaller.
A sense of detachment thrives
in the shadowless twilight.
Ant hills, impenetrable cathedrals, rise
over brittle bushes.
Annoyed by flies, cattle flip their tails,
rub against a high stump.

10

Tents pitched in a mango grove.
Bickering cooks.
Strong box chained
to one of the cots and poles.
The administrator from Sokoto
assigned the unmapped areas,
distributed aerial survey photos,
and drove off with his catamite.
Somebody should tell the watchman
he doesn't have to heave bricks
to disperse the crowds
that come around to stare;
the mute surpliced choir
at every campsite; the traders
displaying their jewelery,
flyswatters and red leather satchels,
wiping kiwi shoe polish
on their ebony statues;
the students eager to practice English.
Makeshift fence around the latrine.
Lanterns primed.
Cold white men slumped in canvas chairs,
writing, reading, stoking the fire;
and in the fading day, the dusty tantrum,
the wind trying to grab the light
and falling back on the unplanted ground.
Beethoven has replaced The Stones
on the portable record player,
batteries running low as the sun sets.
Solitary rider in black and gold cape
appears on a caparisoned stallion
prancing across the soccer field.

II

Another invitation from the emir
to come over for a few beers
at ten in the morning.
Kerchiefs, embroidered caps
blown high above the street.
Undecorated calabash bowls stacked
next to dented, white Mercedes
at the entrance to his compound.
And what looks like a Savonarola chair.
Workmen have just finished repairing the wall
and stand before it, drawing
imbricated rows of arcs
across the still wet mud
with their outstretched fingers; a pattern
of grooves to ward off sun and wind.
This old village should move away from itself,
he says, a mile or two down the road
away from the sewage which has permeated
its foundations. Tribal scars
lost in his wrinkled face, his village
dying since the new highway bypassed it,
young people leaving for the cities,
the European doctors unable to cure him,
his oldest son a pompous dolt.
Tell me, are American albinos
whiter than our albinos?
Lukewarm beer out of the bottle.
Flies.
Boys with shaved heads.
The village scribe will help correct
any misspellings on the new maps.

Why don't you carry a rifle
or at least a pistol
when you go into the bush alone?
Your noisy bike won't frighten a boar
or a bush cow and there are places
you can only get to on horseback.

12

Hundreds of people line the main street
of Dambarta, wave and applaud
as you ride off to work.
. . . Rerouted road intersecting original track;
sections: alternately paved or laterite.
Scattered, temporary settlements.
Estimated populations: below 60.
Dirt trails narrowed down to paths;
condition: seasonal.
Mark them all on the revised map.
Prominent hills, deep ravines,
diverted rivers, damaged bridges.
Photographs useless after a while,
map not much help either;
the spaces between symbols grow wider,
fine dots sprinkled around a thin,
broken line indicate where monotony verges
on change before sinking ahead
in colorless, unbroken waves.
Late start, umbrella of sunlight sprung open.
Permanence and isolation, the aura
of ordinary things in the sand.
Everything a detail.
A tire. A coke bottle.
Shining lengths of pipe
near a rebuilt culvert.
As if they were always there. A strap. A crate.
Details unmoved while mountains were washed away.
Familiar relics on the windswept seabed.

13

Horse panting, ride her into a creek,
a shaded pool up to her shanks.
Stamping as she stood there,
testing her footing?
But she stomps, spooked, rearing
high and ready to bolt.
Must be snakes, can't control her,
wild-eyed and lunging,
can't hold on when just as quickly
she's calm, snorts and trots out,
follows a goat path uphill.
Hot and thirsty, more or less lost,
head throbbing . . . children's voices,
a Protestant mission on the other side of the hill.
Corrugated roofs, generator shed.
Students pet the horse after she loped
into the courtyard, tend to her as you dismount
and knock; female voice, American,
from behind the dark screen.
Footsteps and then she's back, opening the door
just enough to pass through a glass of water.
Thin-lipped pale face. Red head.
"Leave it there when it's empty,"
was all she said.

14

Cane stalks shining in moonlit fields
and the dry riverbed forked across
an imagination where lightning
could scar the land like that.
After a while, it became a ritual
to walk out at night and watch
the silver foxes scamper over the furrows,
kicking dirt into the air, digging
burrows, and then disappear
if a twig snapped underfoot.
And then there was nothing
to do but listen to the fruit drop
from the trees.
Or go to the village and see
the Juju man perform: mumbling,
shuffling in a circle, drinking palm wine
and chewing his medicine;
stabbing his thighs with a sharpened horn
to prove the concoction's power,
and then smiling, invincible in the torchlight,
ankle-deep in a dust pond,
as he showed everybody in Dutsin-Ma
the bloodless cuts deep in his legs.

15

A barber seats you on a curb in Katsina,
scrapes your dry face
with a dull blade and praises the British.
He fought with them in Burma
against the Japanese: The Stealthy Japanese.
I helped capture a platoon one evening.
We pretended we would eat them one at a time,
then let the most nervous escape
so he could tell his officers
and they would all fear us
more than we feared them.
He rolled up his shorts
to show the wound from that campaign,
scar still clear on his leg
where a friend accidentally stabbed him,
diving with a bayonet fixed on his rifle
into the same foxhole
where he had taken shelter
during a bombardment.
Do you know "bombardment?"
Do you know "obliteration?"
It is a British word.
We, my friend and I, had the same marks on our faces
and came from the same village.
Do you know "identity?"
You understand I would be lost without it.
You must tell me, why you smoke
those cigarettes?
They are a poor man's brand.

16

Runka. Men in white caps, white smocks
on the trails to the salt field, sandaled feet
splashing in sand cooled by the night air;
goats crying like infants, the whine
and honk of burros fucking soon after dawn.
Bucket of dried eggs and some bottles of beer
delivered by two girls, gifts from the local emir.
Moving like a wad of gum freeing itself
only to get stuck again, a chameleon
finally dips a slender branch to the ground.
Children with bad teeth, trays balanced
on their heads. A mountain, a huge pile
of boulders behind the village. Gargoyle monkeys
pop out of the clefts and caves to watch
you climb; savannah view expanding with each step,
faded checkerboard fields and riverbeds splayed
under the simmering vagueness of the horizon,
imaginary surf falling far short of a real island
tapered, buttressed in the sun's glare.
On the peak, the sunburst,
spiny silver reaching through the blue,
suddenly erupting, sprouting hawks
that dive for your eyes,
chase you off, down, one arm over your face,
the others swinging a stick,
wings slapping around your ears.

An oven made by packing mud
around discarded fuel drums.
A tongue for breakfast.
Unsliced, lying in the tin bowl
as if it had just pronounced its last syllable.
Three dried eggs. Powdered milk. Coffee.
By the third cup and cigarette, the metallic
sound of shaking leaves that hadn't felt rain
in months, herdsmen in the distance
running behind their flocks.
Thunderheads, black and purple, charging fast
over the horizon, wind sweeping the rain
ahead of them and dust clouds flying
up into the sky like a wish
to join the wind and be taken to the sea.
Jumped on the cycle and drove into it,
grass flattened as if by a wave,
ground turning instantly to mud
which spewed in a rooster tail off the rear wheel;
and when blinded by the rain
you turned and raced the clouds back
to the mountain, the rocks,
and nearing it, the lightning struck just then—
a soundless white burst of time
into which everything vanished but you.

18

Solitary, usually standing
motionless on the outskirts of a market
or beside a main road.
Hair heavily matted, mop-like.
Skin coated with a fine gray ash,
a uniform tone, without a wrinkle
or defined muscle.
No tribal scars, no charms, always alone.
They all looked alike,
softer than a woman,
not squinting in the sunlight,
not heeding any nearby shade,
naked or just from the waist down.
Neither asleep nor awake
but filled with a silence
an old man said was
strong enough to carry them off
in a moment like a bubble
or leave them right where they were
with everything else lasting no longer
than the time it took to pass them by.

A string of silver coins across her forehead.
Feel my ripe tomatoes
Drink Coca-Cola
Long Live The President
printed in that order
across the top of her dress.
The arabic lines above the hem
probably say the same.
Every other kid in the schoolyard
named Muhamed or Ahmadu or Mama or Momo.
Tired, shackled prisoners, a road gang.
Worn blue uniforms soaked with sweat.
Drop their sledgehammers
and rest on the stones they've broken.
Some of them watch a Tuareg family
cross the new highway
on two lurching camels
lashed together like a catamaran.
They usually speak French, Tuaregs,
dislike manual work, leave it
to their wives. When they arrive
in a city they're wanted as night watchmen
since thieves won't go near them.
. . . Swords at their sides,
hands resting on the hilts,
wallets dangling on strings around their necks
outside their billowing robes,
two of them saunter down the sidewalk,
faces covered except for their eyes;
people giving them plenty of leeway:
Tuaregs? you ask Momo,
as if there could be no mistake.
No, he say, they are the Tuaregs' slaves.

Six farmers sharing a pot of rice.
Tuareg beneath a tree
weaving rope with his fingers and toes,
sword in a leather scabbard
hung from a notch in the bark.
Young Fulani leaning on his staff,
watches his herd bump into each other
while they scrounge for grass.
A frail man, rheumy eyes, wet lips,
red teeth on a face masked with dust,
arranges glass and nails on the pavement
and walks down the road
toward Don Gora, places his air pump
and tire repair kit on a square cloth,
hunkers down and waits for the next car;
around his head a ring of flies
which he seems to spin himself
with the cow-tail switch
he methodically flips over his shoulders.
Fresh cobra skin tacked
on the wall of the station house.
Bukar chases a chicken through the yard.
Flies racing around the room,
largest one still winning after five minutes.
A boy hurries by the window, trotting alongside
his burro, jabbing its belly with a stick.
Momo enters: prim and proper, in uniform.
One of the camp workers, the youngest, with him.
He wants some vitamins
and mumbles, hesitates, when asked why.
Momo tells him to drop his pants.
He's wrapped a ball of gauze around his prick;
unravels it, yard after yard
and then points to the leaking chancres
as he counts them: 1 2 3.

Bumpy night flight from Lagos to Kano.
Seats and partitions removed
when the Ibo refugees were being evacuated
so more of them could fit in the plane.
Inept pilots, mostly Indians.
A tendency to land in the wrong city
now and then. A flock of nuns in white habits.
A few ex-pats, hadji and tired
pockmarked women with sleeping children.
Plane suddenly hot, passengers wiping
their faces and eyeglasses, then complaining,
nervously chewing nuts and seeds.
Stewardess races to the cockpit, pilot
and co-pilot burst through the curtain
and run wide-eyed, madly to the rear.
Everyone straining to see what they're doing
jabbering and hammering at a cabinet back there.
Plane suddenly gets cold, unbearably cold.
People shivering, stuttering, pulling
more clothes out of their luggage.
Condensation forming on the ceiling
dripping down on the rich men, the hadji
in lace robes who have been praying in the aisle.

22

This bar in Malamfashi that sold cold beer.
Few sullen girls in the courtyard
and the owner, a big woman with a gold tooth
or two, a necklace of monkey paws
and skin like blue coal, aglow with the dye
that rubbed off her robe.
Circling the tables, collecting green bottles,
she finds a full one, brings it over
and takes the first swig:
"Deluxe," she confirms, "certifiably deluxe!"
Tuaregs wear robes like hers, buy them
in Kano, in a lot pitted with small craters
brimming with the dye; the heavy cloth dipped
and stirred, soaked, rinsed, and pounded with mallets
until they're dry and stiff with a faint, uneven sheen.
You trip over hers on the way
to her room. A low, unlighted arcade.
"Duplex," she says, unlocking the door, "Duplex!"
Her pet rabbits' cool, quivering noses
inspecting your ankles when you enter.
And they jump in bed when she does,
hopping over your neck and back,
sweat wiped off on their long white fur.
Robe on the floor. Dark smudges that rubbed off
on your skin. Shadows across the beams
and thatched ceiling. Rabbits asleep on your chest.
Trip over the nightwatchman on the way out,
who still refuses to wake up
when you start the bike.
Daylight seeping through the trees.
Cameo vultures walking on the road;
vultures will eat so much they get too heavy
to fly, to move out of the way
of the motorcycle
. . . feathers in your spokes.

23

Haul the bike out of what you thought
was the shore of the lake
but had ever so gradually realized
(the horizon rising, leaning toward you,
the earth gracefully reversing its spin)
was a strong mesh of weeds extended
over the surface and sinking
under your weight. The muffler sizzling,
then the quick drop
and another sound that could have been
your soul making a nest in your ear
as the water and fear collared you.
Sit on the hard bank afterward;
maps in the saddlebags ruined.
Think about contracting a disease
(schistosomiasis, a.k.a. "schisto") and watch:
an endless column of brand new ants
ride a conveyor belt out of the ground,
storks motionless in the far reeds,
vultures launched out of the sunset,
a prized digger hat
blown away
on a lake that wasn't on the map.

24

Lebanese merchant guzzles an orange soda.
Two policemen in sharply creased blouses
and shorts pedal back to Katsina.
Hazy, windless acres, the marketplace.
Vultures, hundreds of them, descend
to forage among the locked stalls
and lean-tos and mount
the swept-up piles of scrap.
Momo quotes Plutarch:
People once believed the bird came
full grown from some other world
because a fledgling vulture was seldom seen.
And Hercules always considered
seeing one before an important event
a lucky omen because they were good-natured
creatures, they never damaged fruit trees
or corn or preyed on any living thing
and never touched another bird
even if it was dead.
He raises the volume of his new transistor
when he sees her: a Fulani girl
with hair braided into long, thin loops
and ankles steeped in metal bracelets,
totes a stack of unsold calabash bowls
out of the marketplace; sweat
trickling between her small breasts.
An older, snaggle-toothed girl
with mesmerizing eyes and a baby slung
in the robe around her waist
approaches her and they begin reciting
the standard greetings
before they're 20 feet apart:

How're your cattle, how're you, your father,
your mother, your brothers and sisters,
your sister's husband, your mother's sisters,
your mother's sisters' husbands . . .
and without breaking stride
they pass each other
still going down the list
even when out of earshot.

25

Pass the boulders where a family
of baboons had been earlier today.
Huge, muscular backs, grim faces
slowly turning to look at
you slowly backing away.
Tonight the sand is snowbright.
No time to have put the muffler
back on the bike. A few lanterns on
at the mission. Watchman asleep
across the doorway of the main building.
No sooner does the nun hear
that Randy's temperature is 105
and climbing than she's grabbed her satchel
and hopped on the bike.
Holding on with one arm,
warning the shortcut isn't a good idea.
Her white robes flying in the moonlight
and then later dissolving in the bushes
when she had to go ahead on foot.
Both tires flat, riddled by thorns.

Mourners marching under black umbrellas.
Body wrapped in white cloth,
open straw casket
carried through a street in Ungogo.
Ibrahim maneuvers the truck around them,
nudges a burro out of the way
and bounces over a curb, crushing
his red fez against the cab roof.
The station house unoccupied for years.
The emir sends a few men
to clean it out, sweep up the bat shit
and shoot the cobras.
All the gear unpacked by sundown.
A rat scurries out the door
and dives into a pile of stones,
tail sticking in the air, too fat to hide.
Bala laughs and drops his spear,
wraps the tail around his fist
and whips it out. Yusufu, peering over his shoulder,
gets smacked right in the face with it,
staggers back as Bala dashes it against the wall.
. . . Walk to the High Life club after dinner.
Army officers treating everyone to Star beer.
Musicians crowding the stage:
sax, trombones, trumpets, clarinets:
70, 80 dancers, 4 or 5 abreast,
women singing, men shouting the refrain,
holding each other's waist,
squirming hips under tie-dye dresses, merry
giant caterpillar led by a dented trumpet
around the tables and bar.
That man clenching pieces of glass in his hand,
why is he chasing you?

This man plenty old.
He be Sudan Man.
He speak English small-small, his arm
bending as the bow bends,
short, trembling bow and long, thin arrow.
He finally shoots and the bird drops
squawking in the brush.
Trustworthy, diligent, totally reliable,
fine with children, neat,
punctual old men from Chad or the Sudan
wearing tweed jackets over their robes,
unwrap a precious sheaf of recommendations
in English or French; wrinkled, discolored,
taped at the creases, some dating back
30 or 35 years, some noting
the cuisines they've mastered.
Pockmarked, a young man
in a dacron suit and lacquered shoes
(swollen navel that's prevented him
from joining the army
protruding like a doorknob
through his open shirt)
presents letters of reference
to strangers outside a new store;
some illegible, some obviously forged.
Not as many openings now
as there were after the Ibo were driven off
or killed; mobs roaming from one
ex-pat's house to the next,
hunting the servants
hidden in the attic or under the porch,
dragging them out to the yard,
stabbing them over by that generator.

Shaved heads bobbing through quiet alleys.
Men crammed in the back of open trucks,
hands shielding their eyes.
Bala and Yusufu in heavy woolen caps
pulled over their ears,
quit mending the tents to eat lunch.
Momo, the brim of his digger hat pinned up
with a brass insignia, advises you
not to share the meal because a gentleman
shouldn't mingle with laborers.
An angry youth with a Dutch fisherman's cap
pulled low over one vacant, bulging eye,
disrupts the conversation
by accusing you of being a spy.
Palm wine—brought from a lanky old man
under a straw parasol of a hat—tastes vile,
almost too thick to drink.
Swallow it anyway, smoke some india hemp,
end up drawing on the plaster wall:
a wildebeest mounting the girl
wearing a striped kerchief.
Can't erase it all in the morning
before Ali the cook arrives with a new hula
that Ali the nightwatchman knitted for him.
One village in this section's map
is nameless since everyone there
thought you were a game warden
and ran away when you rode into it,
not stopping to retrieve the white caps
that fell off as you chased them
through the woods; not about to ride
fifty miles back there either;
but your sister's name sounds authentic,
it's her birthday
so name the place after her.

Surprised how fast this old guy can run.
Speedometer topping twenty
and he's still five feet
ahead of the front wheel;
heels flashing, nearly kicking himself in the butt.
. . . Poachers on the straight edge
of the forest preserve.
There they were
loading wood onto backpacks.
Lost again, just wanted to ask directions;
but as soon as they heard the bike
they dropped the blunt axes
and scattered.
Nothing else to do.
Shifted into second and chased them . . .
Catch up to him without hitting third.
But it's not a game to him.
Shift into neutral and stop.
Watch him skitter into the brush.
Lean on the handlebars and look around.
All the stunted leafless trees.
Untie the bandanna, soak it again.
Black rocks and thorny scrub. Solitude.
Long, claw-like white thorns.
Windshreds.
Threshold, where the earth
has yielded all it will
and lost its scent.

30

The sticks, so they burn slowly,
placed like spokes in the sand;
just the tips smoldering in the center.
No work today.
Can't see farther than fifty feet.
Sun a silver smudge.
A nudge of cows,
piebald goats hung like ornaments
in the dense gray air.
Wonder what color the sky will be tomorrow.
Sleepy eyes focusing on the short flame.
Mumble good mornings into a coffee cup.
Men clutching blankets
step squinting out of the tents
onto the decks of fog-bound ships.
The young girl stoops, two big men
hoist the jug from under the spigot
and put it on her head;
erect, eyes gliming its weight,
she turns and walks off
or fades, ascendant, into the ashen day.
Sounds from the village: women
pounding corn, husking peanuts.
Mice have gnawed the erasers
off every pencil.
Ibrahim thinks it is a luxurious habit,
the way you write on only one side of the page.
He can't figure out
what you're doing here anyway
when you could be in America
making $540,000 a year.

Outside the old city: the Sabon Gari,
the Ibo neighborhood; deserted new houses
with sharp corners, tin roofs.
Books lying in the spacious, dusty streets.
Slogans painted above doorways
LOVE ALL   TRUST FEW
Dry open sewers, a wavy line
of bullet holes across a smooth wall.
Staved-in doors. Ransacked rooms.
And on the other end of Kano, right outside
the old city wall's eroded embrasures:
mass, unmarked graves
and past them, more fields, mud compounds,
bundles of firewood, children with bad teeth,
trays of yams carried on their heads,
ubiquitous goats, laterite roads,
culverts, paved roads, another city,
an airport and a cocktail lounge
with a group dressed in western suits,
Yoruba and Hausa men who wanted to talk politics
and asked why the slaughter
had been indiscriminate, why so many
innocent were shot, replied
when your enemy is a tree
and you must chop it down, my good man,
how can you spare the branches?

32

Sun locks into noon.
Race another American
60 miles to the Yankari game reserve.
Stop when a fuel can falls off his bike
and bounces end over end
down the embankment.
Strapping it back on the fender
he wipes the tiny red beads off his forehead
and stares at his hand,
shocked then almost chortling, amused
that he's been sweating blood.
Get there in time for a swim.
Emerald stream coasting out of a cave
at the base of a high cliff,
flowing noiselessly
under a tunnel of dense limbs and fronds.
Nude girls bathing downstream
chattering like the unseen birds.
Vines to swing on through the sunbeams
and drop into the water,
lie on the bottom, hang on to a root
and forget everything,
look up through the flow at the monkeys vaulting
back and forth in the trees,
scattering the light.

33

Walk back to the bike:
Front wheel wedged in a rotten stump
that was hidden by the tall grass.
A few loose spokes. Clean out the filter.
Jaw bone of an ass on the ground.
Slip it under the brake cables on the handlebar.
Get moving again, breeze
blowing the flies off your scraped knees;
gold, flowing grass and clear sky
coaxing your eyes away from the path again.
Then a distant cloud of dust to the right
and another to the left, moving in,
wild dogs, two packs converging in a cloud,
leaping over the handlebars,
all fangs and spit flying in strands;
grab the bone and swing, batting wildly,
crack it across their snouts.
Snarls and whimpers.
Kick the bike into first,
pop the clutch, noise scaring them,
dance with it in neutral, pop it back,
rear wheel shooting sand into their eyes.
Make it somehow to harder ground,
a little traction . . .
in the clear.
All their tails had a white tip.
Alarm still ringing in your head.
Thumbs blistered, ribs sore,
sound of the motor soon absorbed
in the silence again. Scraggy groves.
Huts grouped at the base of a hill
inside a matted fence. One mud house, new
with a checkered, white-washed wall.

A little kid turns a corner and looks up,
drops a water jar from his head,
bursts out in tears and runs off.
First white man he'd ever seen.

34

Free sales demonstration.
Made it himself out of spare parts.
Muzzle-loading pistol
the length of a sawed-off shotgun.
How can he tell how much powder
to use when he's pouring it in the dark?
Rams down some newspaper wadding
and then the grape shot
—nuts and bolts, screws and nails and glass.
Jams the ramrod in the barrel.
Finally wrenches it out.
Match heads instead of flint
or percussion caps.
Cocks the hammer with both thumbs.
Points it toward a tree,
puts one arm over his eyes,
turns his head and fires
a booming three feet of yellow flame
and when the smoke clears
there's nothing left of the sapling
but its stump and everybody's relieved
and happy and can't hear
each other laugh.
He reloads it. Your turn.

35

The first time you heard it told
(at the club bar in Zaria)
a man found a green mamba
curled around the handlebars of his BMW
just after he turned on the ignition.
In the second version, a couple
saw the snake in the same position
while driving home from Salah celebrations.
(Tight spot, what.)
In the third version, a man, considerably drunk,
looked down at his handlebars
and jumped off the bike
while going fifty miles per hour.
Stories drifting into the stale smoke
above the snooker tables.
Trophies. Dartboards. Gin and Tonic.
Bingo once a week on the club patio
and old films from the states.
And then there's the one
about the trainload of Ibo refugees
that was doing alright
until it reached Tiv territory
where it was stopped and sent on
to Port Harcourt
with every passenger decapitated.
Loud, edgy Americans and boisterous Welshmen,
Nigerians with a penchant
for the words "fuck" and "bloody,"
German engineers and mechanics, Indians
and obsequious Indians.
A dreary English menu.
A blonde floating in a blue pool.

36

Peddlers with candy and cigarettes
on candle-lit trays
stroll through the rows of scooters
and bikes outside the open air theater.
Inside, young men, many of them with long,
manicured pinkie nails
to advertise the fact
that they don't work with their hands,
talk incessantly to their dates
while the three-hour film, made in Bombay,
ends with the squat hero
and pudgy, pouting heroine
ardently singing a duet for ten minutes
as they slide side by side
down a mountain of snow on their chests.
Crazed bug in the projector's beam.
Subtitles unreadable in the fake, glaring snow
but by the time they reach the bottom
of the mountain they're obviously reconciled
and would embrace
if the Indian censors had allowed it.
A switch thrown a second too soon,
the final crescendo smeared
across the blank screen.
The audience rises, sandals peeling
off the sticky floor with their first steps.

37

Mosquito bites clustered on an elbow
that slipped out of the netting
during the night, bumps
looking more like the domes
of a mosque in an aerial photograph.
Have to look up the word Za-ke
in the Hausa-English dictionary;
thinking again about that old man
who was hanging around the infirmary
yesterday afternoon.
Coffee brewing.
Milky morning light on dirty windowpanes
and Momo limping by with a cane
trying to avoid piles of black manure.
. . . . see him flying again, catapulted
as you somersaulted off the bike,
earth and sky alternately
flashing in your eyes:

brown blue brown blue Momo

screaming overhead,
dropping, a cracked egg
in the middle of the road.
And fifty miles later, at the infirmary,
waiting outside as Momo was shaved, stitched,
and bandaged, that old man
appearing out of the blue,
the anachronistic reverence in his filmy eyes;
repeating the greeting
he probably gave Lugard's troops
sixty-odd years ago, dropping to the ground,
raising both fists in a double salute
saying Za-ke, Za-ke . . . Lion . . .

38

Stranded now that the bike's demolished.
Second one in three months.
Goof-off all day.
Speak the language.
Ask some bare-breasted girls for directions.
Ask them which way is north,
east . . . putting on sunglasses now . . .
south and . . . west.
Write letters. Use aerograms
with embossed postage so the mailmen
can't peel off the stamps
and destroy the letters.
No place to mail them anyway.
Ibrahim says elephants have been seen
south of Sokoto.
Coke, Fanta, and beer
cooled in a tall water jar;
reach in and fish around for a bottle,
pull up a drowned rat.
Spear throwing contest with Bukar. City boy,
he wears a nylon shirt. You win.

39

Fan out and ford the waist-high stream.
Ibrahim easing the truck along
ten feet behind us.
Slow, brown water. Not on the map.
Film . . . ?
Too late. Canister soaked in back pocket.
Would've been good shots, too.
The Salah celebrations in Katsina.
The palace guard firing musketry salvos.
The sultan coming through the gates
with his retinue and slaves.
His body guards.
Sword-brandishing dykes in red uniforms
and blue sashes, yelling their salutes.
A tourist carried to an ambulance
after a horse stepped on his foot.
Camels and Cadillacs, mock battles on horseback.
And the letter ruined, too.
From Eddie. He's stationed around here.
Teaching or digging wells. An American negro,
unable to go anywhere alone
because he looks Ibo.

40

Quiet, hollow noon.
Thousands of gleaming bicycles
stacked near the mosque.
Black-and-gold flies
buzzing the motionless crowd.
Then the muezzin hollers
through the loudspeakers
and muttering the refrain
an acre of white-robed men sinks
as they kneel, lean down,
press their heads to the ground
and rise again, blinking eastward
with a patch of dust on their brows.
Everyone wore handwoven hats.
Try not to squash anyone's fingers
or leave a footprint on a prayer mat.
Step ashore finally, walk to the bus station.
Sit in the rear and pretend not to see
a clutch of beggars
wiping the dust off the windows.
Three passengers aren't wearing watches.
Women's bracelets jingling with the bumps.
Covered with flies or pox, children
asleep or screaming, laden with charms.
The driver stops for two roadblocks.
The doctors and soldiers
try to inoculate everyone
but some of the young are too well hidden
beneath baskets and satchels
or stuffed under the seats.

41

Blue, red, yellow sheets,
clothes drying on the riverbank
strewn for hundreds of yards in the grass.
Lepers begging at the market gate,
young, old, noseless, blind, crawling
or on crutches they surround
the arriving scooters and bikes
with unexpected speed and shove
their stumpy palms over the handlebars,
demanding Dash me, Bature!
Dash me one shilling!
Fling a pocketful of pennies
over your shoulder, peel out
when they stumble after them
and within you a leaf drops
through vortiginous spaces,
a light is lost in the glare,
the night crowd pushes and carries you
out of a sudden blankness
surf-like through the stalls and wagons,
vegetables and fruit gleaming
under lanterns and candles,
piss and perfume in the dusky air,
mute faces under a canopy of voices,
the bargaining raucous or casual,
hands grabbing or touching, reaching
into the tumult, the cornucopia spilled
here daily between the city and the fields,
carried off on the heads of the tidal crowd;
strangers' conversation changing
to English or French or whatever they guess
you are when you walk by glancing at different
items in the stalls: shoes, tin,

herbs, tools, scrap and spare parts,
bottles, knives, sacks of grain, goats,
homemade pistols, mirrors and lamps,
monkeys, monkey paws, pelts, combs, bolts
of cloth, jewelry, medicine, snake heads
or hides, bright powders, painted tin bowls
all placed, stacked, piled, or lined up
before the tucked-in legs
of large women sweating under a low roof.

42

Bala winces as he files his pointed teeth.
The watchman throws a stone
at someone and misses. Twice.
Horse skull on the edge of an oily puddle.
Simpering monkey on a leash.
Truck stuck.
Children with stained lips, thin
children with worm-bloated bellies,
trays of fish on their heads.
Sky solid blue.
A line of figures seen in the distance
through the wavering heat
seems tenuous, dislodged.
White goats. Flies collide.
Two hawks whistle
and glide and one of them drops
like a stone into the fields.
Crumpled packs of Three Rings
tossed on the floor.
An incomplete tic-tac-toe pattern
on a painted façade in the village.
Bird tracks cover the dusty plaza.
Giraffes have whiskers.
Sun about to set, white and round,
rounder than the third *o* in monotony.
Take a bath.
Climb back into the same dirty clothes.

43

Green light of a full moon.
Sokoto to Kano to the Jos Plateau,
wind stretching your face, bike roaring,
tracing roads between city lights
afloat in the darkness, lights
of a constellation that will finally end
when you follow time past it to sleep,
out of its midst, to some distant village
where maybe a language is spoken
that uses the same word for a well
as for a woman's eyes, for clarity
drawn from darkness, song from thought.
Gravel splattered from the wheels
of oncoming trucks, lopsided, loaded,
with bales of cotton, sacks of peanuts;
dragon-like, the headlight beams,
the smoky grinning grills.
Taking curves at higher speeds
you widen an edge
that was no thicker than your shadow.
Instant dawn:
the day opens its red gate.
Night and day, which chases which?
A seclusion in speed,
the silence of heights from where you watched
clouds race their shadows to the shore,
cloud raining on its shadow,
rain falling white in the sunshine.

44

Stony fields,
full moon,
skinny traveler
getting skinnier.
A cold fart near the Niger border.
Sandals made from old tires.
The left one from a white-wall.
Intermittent fever. And the sweat:
whatever is dissolving inside.
Shivering interrupted by shakes;
body trying to shake you off.
Days slower as the savanna
nears the desert; villages smaller,
shrinking. Idle girls, naked, giggling,
covered with dust and beaded shells.
Children want to touch your hair.
Silhouettes turning to splotches
in the long twilight, the road
seems to lift, drifting off the ground
and the wind falters like a voice
wandering past the end of a song.
Purifying pills make the water
taste dry, then you hear it fall
into your empty stomach,
then you begin this dance you do
when there's no one else around for miles.

45

A lorry finally leaving Zinder,
its cab decorated with mirrors, fringe, and rugs.
Tuaregs scramble aboard like pirates,
indigo robes, swords in red sheaths,
fighting politely for room.
Metal sheets full of holes attached alongside,
to be shoved under the wheels
if they got stuck in the sand.
Goat skins and old inner tubes
bulging with water.
No sooner started, then stopped to pray.
Drive through the night,
a boy singing constantly.
Spend the afternoons under the lorry
or thorn bushes that cast the shadow of a web;
sharing water, speechless in the heat.
Oil drums placed a mile apart
to mark the sand-swept tracks.
Arrive at Agadez, wondering if it's still
possible to cross the Sahara.
Told each morning: Yes, a truck tomorrow,
a truck tomorrow . . .
Then the Arab-Israeli war began
and no Americans permitted in Algeria.

46

Agadez. A place to wait.
Ostrich caged in the town square.
Magpies perched on the minarets
streaked with their white droppings;
wax running down a candle.
Desert north of the town.
Stroll away, immersed in silence
when the war reports and static
from radio loudspeakers
grow fainter and the sun fills half the sky.
In the afternoon, people and sheep
walk close to the walls; children with bad teeth,
trays of yams carried on their heads,
wade in rare shadows.
But at night it's cool, sleep outside,
listen to the breeze drop now and then
like the dream of a wave
through the dry trees.
Try to trace some constellations.
The Cross of Agadez leaning northward
over the maze of houses and walls.
The dogs howling.

47

After five days someone heading south
in a fuel truck with room
for one more in the cab.
' He spoke pidgin small-small,
he be Sudan man.
Road reduced to tracks and ruts,
steering wheel jumping out of his hands.
Ostrich running in the distance,
old people seated alone
beside the road now and then;
he stopped once, for a woman
begging for water with a cracked bowl.
She kept her head down, one hand over her eyes
while he poured and they didn't speak
to each other. Back in the truck,
shifting gears again, he said
they were all too weak
to move with their people, that they would
die there far from the wells
. . . where the tribes gathered,
water level lower every day,
stones bounced off the ribs of trudging oxen,
rope and rigging readjusted after each team
drew up the boat-sized leather buckets
and the water was doled out to the crowd . . .
He stopped at a place called In-gal
and he wanted to be paid for the ride
with vitamin pills instead of money.
Tipped him a few aspirin.

48

Somewhere the rivers are slowing down,
are less and less deep every year
and will soon be shallow enough to lie on
and let the water pour over you as you sleep;
the birds don't panic at dawn
and walk more than they fly; the ocean
sends one less wave ashore every day,
one more thought of sleep.
Fine dust above the goat paths
suspended in the sunlight,
then drifting upward
as though the ground were raining on the sky.
The network of goat paths lining the ridges
and mounds which were once the city walls of Kano.
Sunlight, the memory of it, entering
the arid space of a demolished building in New York.
Dreamy movements of light and dust.
A slow shadow revolving at the center
of flattened miles,
one ant dancing with a dead ant in the sand.

49

Foliage burgeoning in summer rain
or so you remember, watching
tea leaves unfurl at the bottom of a cup,
and imagine it all gone, the scenery,
not eroded but erased in a soft breeze.
Stray details remaining, superimposed
in the air like a gift; the stark things
found out there in the sand: a tire,
a shoe, a coke bottle, appear new, untouched
while everything around them
has been blown away; a single recollected object
in a scene that otherwise eludes remembrance.
Flies on a silver plate.
White sun melting behind branchless trees.
Chimney smoke yanked out of visibility.
Shadows pulled toward the oncoming night.
You wipe the grime off the window
and then off your hands.
A cloud looks snagged on a tree.
Spring water flows off like excess clarity.
In the village, the women never stop
to take a breath, but sing
with the ease of a stream,
of the earth ceaselessly emptying itself.

· *Tryptych* ·

Tryptych

MORNING

6:30   (2)   Sunrise
        (4)   Knowledge
        (5)   Comparative
              Geography
        (13) Images and Things
        (71) Listen and Learn
7:00   (2)   News
        (4)   News
        (5)   WIDE WORLD
        (8)   Public Affairs
7:30   (4)   Young Africans
        (9)   Elsie Aquacade
        (10) The Young and
              the Restless
        (13) Religious
              Humoresque
        (71) Espionage
8:00   (2)   Asian Dimension
        (5)   To Be Announced
        (6)   VANISHING POINT.
              A Sentinel in
              Swamplight; snow
              falling on black
              mud.
        (10) WEATHER. Flood
              footage, birds
              hop from branch
              to branch as the
              water rises
              higher and
              higher.

8:30   (8)   PERIPLUM
        (9)   Mr. Itchy Starlight
        (11) DUENDE. He
              drives into a
              tree, he listens
              to the apples
              bounce off the
              hood of his car.
8:45   (9)   WEATHER.
              Thunderclaps,
              the clouds
              stampede.
        (10) SUBMISSION
9:00   (2)   Bugs Bunny
        (7)   Snorkeling with
              Captain Bravo
        (8)   TALES. "Why all
              this fear and
              trembling," said
              the Wizard to
              the Shrew, "is
              life all you
              know?"
9:30   (80) Violence in Blue
        (4)   Lisping Marauder
        (71) El Reporter
10:00   (7)   SERMON. What
              part of paradise
              is made of
              memory.

(9) SCIENCE.
A hammock rope
is tied around a
tree; as the
trunk grows the
bark swallows
the rope and
leaves an
interesting
scar.

10:30 (13) MODERN
EXPLORATION.
The space a
seemingly
mindless, rush-
hour crowd
leaves around a
raving idiot.

(71) BLINDSPOT

11:00 (2) FANFARE. Blood
on a concrete
piano.

(4) LOVELORN.
Figure on a
mountaintop
digging up
seashells.

(5) Dragonquest

(7) Elizabethan and
Nova Scotian
Music (with
Charles North).

11:30 (9) FEATURE.
Telling fortunes
by burning
seaweed.

(13) MUTINY. Fog
drifts up to the
house and
crashes through
the windows.
Elephants bark
in the distance.

(71) FUTURAMA

AFTERNOON

12:00 (4) News

(7) NEWS AND WEATHER.
The wind hunting
silence.

(8) INQUISITION

12:30 (2) A CHILLING TALE.
A man with long
blond hair
hands a
threatening note
to a teller with
long blonde
hair.

(13) MODERN
EXPLORATION.
A deer trying to
climb a ladder.

(71) NECROPOLIS

(6) INTERLUDE.
Poisoned rats
rot in the
walls. You
vacuum large
black flies
off the screens.

1:00   (5) WHITE STRAWBERRIES

       (7) SNORT. No war buff, me.

       (8) Damaged Perspective

       (9) APPLIANCES AT AN EXPOSITION

      (10) Smut

1:30   (6) TIME SPAN. "... and the spiders were singing in the wells."

     (71) SCIENCE. An examination into the earwax of various races. Curious results.

     (80) WEATHER. Bleak snowlight, black helicopters to the rescue.

1:45   (4) Dream Overload

      (5) A Stack of Bibles

2:00   (2) VIGIL. 8 people on a train platform reading little books.

      (4) DISCOVERY. My elbow, the left one, the first time I've noticed it in years. Highlights: scars from unremembered wounds, new hair.

      (5) Polyphemus

     (13) LA HISTORIA. The men in Columbus's crew are allotted over two liters of red wine per diem.

2:30   (6) MOSTLY PROSE. A bug flies through my eye. The crowd cheers.

      (8) CHERISHED FORMS

3:00   (7) Conquistador

     (13) MODERN EXPLORATION. Spaces in the air where the wind waits disguised as silence.

4:00   (4) JUMPING JESUS

      (5) Split Second

4:30   (6) VANISHING POINT. And I sink through the chilly rain and leafless trees, past the colorful clothes left out on the line.

(8) SPORTS AND
WEATHER. Click.
Clunk. People
bowling in the
fog.

5:00 (2) HOMILY. A long-
lost color
returns to earth
in a fleet of
of clouds, ending
millennia of
heretofore
inexplicable
melancholia.

(9) BITCH ON WHEELS
6:00 (2) Hitleresque
(13) ARCHAEOLOGY.
Pillars strewn
wowie-zowie
across the sea
floor of a
sunken palladium.
(71) RALPH WONDERFUL
(80) Bucharest
7:00 (2) News
(4) Cow with hair-
lip: Moof.
(7) NEWS AND
WEATHER.
Intermittent
gales which
drown the
crickets, 100s
of acorns hit
the roof and
roll down the
shingles.

EVENING

7:30 (13) BRAHMS. Piano
Concerto 2 in B
flat major.
(45) Pythagoras
8:00 (2) UPDATE. The
magicians
explain why they
failed.
(9) SOUVENIR. A
pubic hair, a
perfect 6, on a
bar of soap.
9:00 (7) Art which was
not interested
in motion or
time.
(9) HOUR OF BLISS
(11) STRANGE
ENCOUNTER.
"Neither
darkness nor
light," said the
swamp angel,
"Neither darkness nor
light can fill
my eyes."
10:00 (2) CUISINE. Does
torn bread
really taste
better than
sliced bread?
(8) Black Dimes
10:30 (7) MY BLOOD RAN
COLD

(9) THE YOUNG
ELPENOR.
Besotted, he
falls off roof,
breaks neck,
dies. The sea-
dark wine.

(11) KARMA. The live
leafless
branches and the
dead tree
against the sky,
all grappling
with the wind.

(71) TIME AND
TOLERANCE. An
invisible nude
enters the
elevator. She's
chewing gum.

11:00 (2) Moon out of
focus

(5) INTERMISSION.
She leaves the
table, her
elbows are wet.

(6) Cloud Armada

(8) Hours bubbling
in the
everlasting wake
of paradise.

(11) CANYON. Another
herd faceless
and innumerable
rushes by

without showing
Biff and Sally
the way out.

11:30 (5) SURF. Waves
wearing warbonnets
charge a pair of
plump identical
twins.

(6) FIFI FLEES—FOUL
PLAY FEARED.

(8) TYPICAL
BAUDELAIRE:
". . . no point is
sharper than
that of the
infinite."

12:00 (2) LUMINARY. In
1903, he turned
his attention to
the east . . .

(9) WATERLOO.
Napoleon loses
because severe
case of
hemorrhoids
prevents him
from
concentrating on
the course of
the battle.

(11) FINISHING
TOUCHES.
A cloud floats up
to the moon and
stops. Jolting
finale avoided.

· King Nasty ·

King Nasty

"Let me sketch it out for you,
off the top of my head.
I'll tell you what I want,
you fill in the blanks.
Begin smack in the middle,
the French Revolution, the Reign of Terror,
the glub and gloom of disillusionment,
the mumbo jumbo of annihilation.
Let the gray sets
—sluggish music, sparse dialogue,
mostly grunts and noise—alternate
with the tumult of the daylight crowds,
the din, the frenzied color,
all bellow and froth.
Open with a long shot, Place de la Concorde.
Move in over the rooftops and skylights,
troops and proclamations.
Aim at the headsman.
He's at the pinnacle of his career,
tromping around the scaffold,
ablaze with sunlight.
Make the scaffold about 100 square feet,
unseasoned wood.
Drop to the prisoner, a skinny runt
tied face-down to a plank.
The headsman looms over him,
the guillotine rig over the headsman.
His boots slip on the blood-soaked deck
as he shoves the runt onto the lock.
I want a high angle shot of the blade,
silver, white, then pan left
until it's lost in the sun.
The blade drops, the crowd cheers.

Now this executioner, he's big, right?
The crowd calls him Big Boy.
He wears a mask that flaps down
over his nose. Large eyeholes.
A black mask, and a leather apron,
beefy arms, a black tooth or two.
Floppy boots, you know the kind.
A snaggletoothed lummox, but professional.
Give him a tattoo: a crown pierced by a dagger.
Did they wear tattoos then?
I think Cook's crew
had brought them back from Tahiti.
Check it out.
Whatever, make sure it's lurid.
You get the idea.

All right. It's noon. The chain rattles,
the blade rises: a slow crank.
Cut to quick shots of the next prisoners.
You ever read Byron's letters, the one
where he describes the executions he saw?
Well, that's what I want.
The first prisoner sobbing;
the second stunned, dumb;
the third sneering, scornful,
still trying to wrench free.
They bind the first to the plank,
lay him down, lock him in.
Another shot of the high rig,
the cross-piece, the blade.
Then its whispering fall
and—thud, the head drops, and bounces,
the legs twitch crazily.
No, wait! Scratch that. I got it.

While the blade rises and all that,
cut to the spectators:
old hags, young damsels, students,
business types, burghers—
you know, the usual crowd scene.
But catch these two fellows taking bets
on how many times the heads will bounce.
Then thud, and a split-second shot
of the neck before it erupts.
A four-foot spray at least.
Oh, hold it. The head has to bounce.
It bounces twice and rolls.
The loser in the crowd curses
and jabs a coin into his pal's palm.
Quick switch to the second prisoner.
His head bounces three times in a long shot.
Again the roaring multitude.
This time the guy wins the bet.

Now the third victim.
Follow Byron to the letter on this one.
A burly man, he struggles all the way.
Big Boy can't close the stock,
can't lock it over the guy's thick neck.
He has to sit on it.
The victim keeps pulling back,
so when the blade hits it takes off his head
just above the ears.
No spurt of blood this time,
just a slow white ooze.
And the top of his head shouldn't bounce,
just flop on the boards like a bowl.
The crowd boos Big Boy,
who is truly annoyed.

The bettors curse and call it a draw.
Through all this, work in a cameo:
The young Goethe, play him up with commentary,
the astute, disinterested observer.
Good chance for exposition here.
End the scene with his pronouncement
that the whole noisome show
displays "a stupidity that defeats the gods."
I also want to see somebody
wretch into a silk handkerchief.
I've always wanted to see that.
And I want poetry in the dialogue,
at least two-and-a-half heaves per line.

Next scene—am I going too fast?—
Early morning dark, misty.
The same place, the plaza empty.
Move in on a few garbagemen
working under the scaffold.
Did you see that film *Danton?*
Well, I didn't either,
but somebody told me about a shot in there
that I want you to copy.
Only make it original.
Two carts with high wooden wheels,
no spokes—or does that sound medieval?
I don't know. Check it out.
These garbagemen, they're grim, they're stooped,
they have broad shovels
and they're scooping up the clotted blood
and straw under the platform,
and dumping it into the carts.
This is a very quiet scene.

The blood is thick and black
and they walk and wobble on it
like Lilliputians on a plate of jello.
Big Boy is working late.
He's talking to an officer.
Clandestine executions in the works.
They're discussing a new delivery,
prisoners packed into a tumbrel,
its wheel rims muffled,
wrapped in burlap.
The officer offers a bribe.
Big Boy resists, none of the prisoners
are on his list, the risk is great, et cetera.
The officer points to the moody goons
guarding the tumbrel
and Big Boy mulls it over and complies,
shoving the money under his apron.
Keep it realistic.
They should speak in French accents,
so give them a shot of Novocain in the lips.

Now, see if you can make this work.
The bribing avengers take over.
Torchlight and twisted faces.
No choreographed slaughter here
but the worst of it: hatred,
wild cruelty, sloppy horrors.
Get it? A little revolutionary excess.
I'll give you my notes on what happened
at Portiers and Lyons
and the September massacre.
Follow that scenario.
Have the goons and zealots
bugger the aristocrats
after they lock them in the guillotine.

Have them signal Big Boy to drop the blade
so the gagged and screeching aristos
die in a boinnnnng-eyed shudder
just as the buggers' frenzy peaks.
Don't overdo it.
Close the scene with something subtle,
artistically redeeming—say,
a wizened crone on the sidelines
quoting Montaigne.

After that, slowly back out of the set.
Mist again, the scaffold in lantern light,
then fog filling it all to a gray blank.
Hold it for a few seconds,
no image but the sound
of slow wings, gradual, heavy flight,
rhythmic, heaving the air aside.
But instead of wings it's a man's arms
swinging as he walks,
his sleeves brushing his coat,
hardly discernible, nearly disembodied.
Then his face—It's Big Boy sans mask,
heading home after a rough day.
Lead him down a side street.
Deep gutters, narrow, filthy, wet.
He opens a low door and enters
a smoky kitchen, dark, colorless.
His wife lugs a kettle to the stove,
pokes around the hearth.
She's glum, harried.
Three glum children, dirty, expressionless.
Big Boy hunches over the table,
thick fingers splayed on the rough boards.
A metal plate under his chin: stew.

Slobbering, he wipes up what's left
with a chunk of bread, wipes it clean
until there's a shadow,
the blur of his reflection on the plate.
—No, cancel that.
But I want a lot of weight.
I want the kitchen to be like a cave.
Everything quiet.
Even the smoke droops.
His wife plops a pair of boots in front of him.
He examines the soles, the new studs.
Now cut to a flashback at the plaza.
The usual faces, sunlight.
Prisoners jammed into a rickety tumbrel.
Right out of *A Tale of Two Cities*.
A dreary parade of tumbrels.
Close shots of the jeering uglies.
Contempt and boisterous condemnation.
Go for the strong contrast
with the prisoners' stupor.
Young, old, priests, poorfolk,
gaunt aristocrats, baffled and weeping.
You know the bit: devastation and woe.
Then a quick series of beheadings:
Chop, chop, chop.
The ballooning shadow of Big Boy
on the smeared planks.
Even his shadow looks bloated.
His boot slips and he falls on his butt.
He's the entertainer, playing the crowd.
The blood thick and thin, curdled and fresh.
Big Boy on tiptoe now.
He yanks a periwig off an aristo's head
and skims it over the waving spectators.

Now—No, hold it. Now I've got it!
One head rolls to his feet.
He looks down and he hears, he sees
the head say something!
The background noise is tremendous
but he's sure he's not deceiving himself.
The head makes a sound.
You've got to catch his incredulity.
Make sure the eyeholes
in the mask are large enough for that.
Hold the close-up.
Now a jump cut back to the kitchen,
where he's at the table, slumped, sullen,
and remembering this as the wife
and children putter around.
This next shot is crucial:
One of the children is drawing on the wall.
She's using pairs of knots
in the wallboards for eyes.
The wasted Big Boy watches her
as she fashions, very delicately,
one face after another.
Another flashback:
Again he sees that head make a sound.
It's not a gurgle, not a gasp,
but a definite word.
Now keep cutting in
with a series of flashbacks,
at least five or six,
in which he recalls other heads
on other days, other victims
who also said something to him.
Cut to the mute child
outlining more faces in pencil.

The pairs of knots portray
every human expression
but mostly downcast, mostly dread.
A lot of faces! Make that wall
look like a whirlwind in the underworld
where nothing is left of the spooks
but their dark eyes, their feelings.
Then keep intercutting the heads
that Big Boy has seen speak.
I need a big build-up here,
maybe something from Beethoven's *Eroica,*
as Big Boy, bristling with revelation,
realizes that all this time
the words that the heads have been uttering
are forming phrases . . .
and that the phrases are on their way
to a sentence . . .
Maybe run all the different heads by
in a montage first,
sweet, horrified, deadpan.
Give each a word as if they were
Burma Shave signs on the roadside
and Big Boy's waking up at the wheel.
First head: "It's . . ."
Second head: "when . . ."
Third: "men . . ."
Fourth: "try . . ."
Fifth: "to . . ."
Sixth: "be . . ."
Seventh: —Cut it off there for now.
Then have Big Boy hear them repeated—
"It's when men try to be . . ." —
by one voice that sounds
like the unimaginable, a cosmic echo,
a god's first scream of disbelief.

You know, lightning
and something else, something red, not thunder.

Yeah, it's far-fetched
but it'll work.
I got the idea from reading
about the German pirate, Stoertebaker.
When the British finally caught him,
before they cut off his head
they gave him a last request.
He said, "Kill me standing up
and spare as many of my crew
as I can run past after you swing the ax."
So, they cut off his head
and he manages to make it past fourteen of them.
What a class guy, a stand-up guy.

Anyway, back to Big Boy.
Jump ahead.
Multitude and spectacle.
Big Boy's back on the job.
He's slowed down, the pace with him.
He's not playing to the masses anymore,
he's more deliberate.
After each head drops, he stares at it,
waiting for the next word in the sentence.
No one else, none of his assistants
is in on this, as more words
seep out of the victims' mouths.
"It's when men try to become angels . . ."
No let up on the procession of prisoners.
All in red smocks.
Get the foreshortened view of the dead,
headless, sprawled, wriggling,
each bound to the plank.

Let's have the winds-of-time-
ripping-pages-off-the-calendar shot
superimposed on the racket.
Stick to the facts.
Make seven out of ten victims peasants,
the rest deputies, journalists, big shots,
Girondists, royals, shopkeepers,
over-the-hill Montagnards.
But you'll have to scramble the chronology.
We're working up
to the execution of the Sun King!
—I said don't worry about accuracy—
and the words from the severed heads
have been piling up:
"It's when men try to become angels that they . . ."

Now the Sun King gets his.
—No, hold off on that.
We need more on Big Boy.
The slaughter is incessant.
"Absolute virtue pursued with absolute terror."
The horror drags him in deeper.
Out of the Pol Pot and into the frying pan.
Big Boy on tiptoe.
Unable to predict when a head
will say something, he stares
ever closer into the doomed faces.
Bring on a few notables.
Whenever one of them gets it,
he expects another word—
if not the word incarnate,
then at least a wink.
Let's set up Robespierre.
Put on your Panorama hat for this one.

A greater crowd than ever.
Banners: Liberty, Equality, Fraternity.
Flocks of doves. Keep it festive.
Robespierre climbs the scaffold,
or have them lug him up.
Big Boy's lackey wrenches off his coat.
His socks, his stockings fallen,
he's an undignified wreck.
But Big Boy's more than disappointed.
Robespierre, he tried to commit suicide
earlier and only managed to shoot off his jaw.
He can't talk.
Big Boy's more than angry,
he's mean, he's foul, he's vengeful.
He rips the bandages off
and throws them to the creeps on the sidelines,
who fight for them like dogs.
The crowd settles down—stillness.
They know what Big Boy has in mind.
He makes Robespierre wait a long time
before letting the blade drop.

So it goes.
We should have at least one
plaza scene in the rain.
Maybe this one—Charlotte Corday.
She must be beautiful, brunette, gentle.
Too gentle to look like
she could have shoved a dagger
even into the pasty, water-logged Marat.
Just what was his problem, anyway?
Eczema? V.D.? Skip it.
This is a pivotal scene.
Big Boy searches her eyes
as if she'll tell him the word
while she's still alive.

According to Carlyle, she blushed
when the headsman removed her kerchief.
That's a nice touch. Use it.
Her head falls—slow motion here—
and sure enough, when he lifts her head
—with both hands, pure melodrama,
he's almost reading her lips—
she pronounces an entire word,
three syllables no less,
that sets him back on his heels.
He swoons: three syllables: "resemble."
"It's when men try to become angels
that they most resemble . . ."

Finally, let's skip ahead.
The Sun King, it's curtains for the Sun King
on the shortest day of the year.
And Big Boy's sunk.
The stress has broken him.
He's been taunted, haunted by his victims,
the flesh made word.
But before that the King
has to give a speech.
And I've got just the line.
I forget which, it was either Louis XIV or XVI
who after losing a battle
said, "Has God forgotten
all that I have done for him?"
I don't care who said it, use it.
Have the King, at his own request,
lie face up, staring high into the glare,
so the blade drops, shoots down
as if the sun exploded.
It's always been a heavy symbol.

The shadow of the blade
hits his throat first.
Slow-motion stop and go.
Big Boy grabs the head by the hair
before it hits the drenched deck
and holds it aloft.
It starts to spin slowly
and he turns with it,
beseeching it, tête-à-tête,
his eyes bulging more
than the dead head's.
The people get more excited believing
Big Boy's displaying it for them.
A tremendous crescendo.
Citizens start to scramble
onto the scaffold, clamoring
to dip their handkerchiefs
in the king's blood.
Big Boy, still awaiting the word,
stamps on their fingers,
tries to stomp them
without taking his eyes off the King.
The crowd bellows and waves,
waves money at him;
those closest to the edge
demand a lock of Louis' hair.
They want to rip his coat apart,
wear strips of it as headbands.
Big Boy refuses, yanks the coat
away from his assistants with one hand.
The crowd begins to jeer him.
Thousands in thunderous unison
take up the disdainful cry,
calling him King Nasty! King Nasty!

. . . King Nasty or King Naughty.
He can't concentrate in the tumult.
He's lost it, he's missed it,
foiled by the bellow and roar
of his own name.
The King says something—
"It's when men try to become angels
that they most resemble . . ."
but Big Boy loses it
like a drop in the ocean.
This has to happen very fast,
absolutely deafening noise
that ends in absolute silence,
ringing silence
with Big Boy staring deaf and dumb
into God knows what.

That's it for today.
I've given you plenty to go on,
try to kick it into shape.
Put your heads together.
Maybe you can find something else
for that sentence. I'm loose.
Maybe you can come up with a palindrome.
Maybe we got a play here.
Or convert it into an opera.
A Musical. Or all three.
We could run a contest.
The heads can sing a jingle.
Think about casting right away.
Ask the sponsors to suggest somebody.
Anyway, that's it.
Let's have a drink.
How do you like your bourbon?

· Wet Bread and Roasted Pearls ·

Wet Bread and Roasted Pearls

Through a filmstrip of train windows,
I watch the river coast by, mist
climb the Palisades to open sky.

Hudson line. Gravel trackbed
dusted with snow, bank rock and piling
blackened with oil, barges
half-rotted on granite slabs
where a deer dips her head in bent reeds

and then steps out onto shore ice:
One long wave of white ice
nightwinds caught at its farthest reach
between arrival and return
and held gleaming above the tide.

The ideogram for "recognition,"
you know, was formed from the figure
of a deer: to leap from a standstill.
And when the thin ice
suddenly collapses
and I see the doe slide, stagger,

but somehow remain on a wobbling piece
that carries her
out into the mist—there's
the ideogram for "amazement":
to be standing in that splendor.

Blue cliffs lean against bluer sky,
blue as the wreaths
around smokers' heads,

sleepers' heads, readers' heads;
blue as the blurred tattoo on his arm,
the old man in the next seat:
the tall ship faded into his skin.

Once across the city line
riverbank turns to rubble.
Row after row of mounds,
a ransacked graveyard
of mistakes buried under broken images,
brick, busted block, scrap metal,
crumpled sheetrock, tires,
charred planks, sand piles
dumped on lots
glittering with crushed glass.

Of the numerous ideograms
for "To fill in the blanks"
one is based on a recognizable figure
heaving gigantic hourglasses
off a train just before it bursts
under a roaring city
and in a quiet tunnel
stalls.

Another contains
a figure, someone who abhors
crossword puzzles, someone
like me, newspaper
in hand, stultified
by a maze of blanks.

Eighty-nine down: More lavish clues.

One across: To be reasonably
suspicious of zeros and words
that contain too many *o*s.

Two across: Prosopopoeia.

Fifty-five down: Monotonous.

Three across: Puzzle is to Mystery
as Grapefruit is to . . .

Five across: Rhymes with orange.

Eight across: Of Aquitaine, as in:

Thirteen across: Of summertime, as in:

I think I'll throw away a poem, take
a nap, and then go stand in the sun.
Or lie beside you on the dock awhile
and write another one.

Or wait for you to open your eyes
and help me figure out
what this little kid on the beach
is all about.

He's pulverized pearls with a rock
after he popped them
like corn in a fire,
a handful of fake pearls
he cast on the water
along with some bread for
Thirty-four down: Type of fish,
a.k.a. "pumpkin seeds."

Crumbs and pearl dust—sunnies
rise out of the murk
like stupidity approaching speech,
then veer off
without a nibble, without a blink.

And, like Twenty-one across:
A magician
who somehow tricks himself,
makes his own charms
disappear, and finds himself
empty-handed in the unyielding air,

the kid just stands there
staring at a puddle of oil
that floats between dock and raft,
its slack colors slipping away
like The Lost Planet, turning
with every move this one ever made.
And whatever made it move:

Gases change to moiling seas,
squashed continent to coastline.
Greenery fades to salt flat
and back again.
Empire and ignorance,
each with its course, its color
—a different color for every age,
every eon, migration and flood,
dust and flood, famine
and soaked plunder, flight
and pursuit, white and yellow
and blue, the aerial swirl of snow
and disease, peace
and convulsion, belief and denial.

And there it goes, sight out of mind,
leaving me

to watch you finally wake
and wonder what dreamt you into being;
to almost know it, but to lose
that, too, in shadow and water,
and then watch reappear
another circling fly, another
'horsefly and gnat, dragonflies
and, Twenty-one down:
The "wizardry in daylight"
that allows them to stay,
suspended
in the ever-expanding sky
that sweeps back
to Thirteen down: Bombay,

where one afternoon, leaving
that city on a slow, quiet train,
trackbed raised
above flooded fields,
no land in sight,
I could see nothing
but sky mirrored in water
and the tremendous sun drawing
its hour-long reflection
across horizonless blue.

Two perfect circles, swirling,
identical,
slid into one, hung there,
where an early world
that greeted the advent of yellow
with flutes and bells
and pure geometry,
intersects Thirty-four across:

The Grapefruit,
the one you thought I'd aimed at you
just because it punctured the wall
next to your ear.
The glaring, almost magical fact of it,
a grapefruit stuck in sheetrock.

One warm afternoon, hillside
yellow with fallen leaves, starlings
began to flock, as plentiful
as the leaves still left in the maples.
All that clatter, so many,
thrown every which way
in the shrapnel wind,
people stepped warily out their door
and wondered what was going on.

Even we, who had seen it before,
could only raise our arms
and laugh at what was as much
a feeling as a sight,
a sound, the sky-blown praise,
the tumult, the soft yellow ground

now as blank as Eight down,
the winter you decided
to freeze me out, kept
the house as cold as a morgue.

Days I didn't hear
you speak except in your sleep,
so that one morning I woke
to the sound of your voice
and a cold draft

and the noisy sparrows
at the window.
I lay there cold and tired
listening to Five down: The first sign
of spring, cheap talk
in the dismal, breaking light.

And when the smoke alarm,
its battery worn down,
began to beep, the signal
at first indistinguishable
from the birdcalls
but then growing louder,
triumphantly monotonous
in their absence, I remained
Three down:
A man of my word.
And that word is
Fifty-five across: Disingenuous.

For the rest of that week
above Peekskill Hollow Road
the ridge loomed, fledged with treetops
rising row behind row.
By the next, the colors
had flown, and for days
in that gray intricacy
of italics and twigs,
the slightest sound reached
a distant, whispered edge: pencil

scraping paper, dry leaves
blown over pavement; a vine
rubbing stone; a piece
of cellophane flying out of nowhere
on that remote lake, skidding
after me as I skated.

And suddenly, as if I were
the figure on the cover
of Two down: A novel
of grim pursuit, regret
and Gothic dread,

there was, inexplicably,
more cellophane,
scraps of clarity, a swarm
of blanks and withered smiles
whirling around me
before I simply turned
and headed back into the wind,
scraping a few more edge-songs
out of what stays, what goes . . .
what happens when we
find ourselves in Eighty-nine across:
An Important Event
in the History of Punctuation:

We lie in the dark and listen.
The window open
you wait for me to guess
what you already know:
that voice so lovely and strange
you can't believe
I don't remember what it is.
And then I do:

Miles of lake ice shift and thaw,
singing the changes
that move as lightly as years
and the lifelong questioning
that keeps turning me toward you

and One down: The origin
of the question mark

in darkness and the curve and line
of your spine, your neck
your chin, your ears, your
legs and breasts and my open hands
—Hands, rough, callused,
sliding over your taut silk
they sound like breath.

· *Sputter and Blaze* ·

Sputter and Blaze

Maybe because you never
did a thing like that before
as invite me to a propeller factory
An idle walk I thought
late night's softened corners
all to ourselves as we passed
through the buzzing gold tent
pitched below each streetlight
you all the while
leading me merrily to the broken gates
the damp the hush the high fence
and I wondering how night or day
I'd never known this place was there
in the middle of a city
a part of you you kept to yourself
a shipyard far from the open sea
a suspiciously quiet factory
A few dim lights in the main shed
ancient cranes and hoists and chains
a few workers wandering around
taking inventory
Checking off two or three
silences for each and every
light and shade of solitude
one for any notion of being
for those parts of ourselves
we only find in silence
or in knowing when someone else
hears the first slow breath a flute
draws from the night sky
and feels the same

The great propellers stacked in the yard
monumental flowers in a field of maybe-nots
drenched with a lightbulb's glow
softer than pollen in the mist
the screw blades gleaming or rusted crimson
Maybe because you had never been there before
you knew we could if we crouched
walk then bee-crawl up
the wide spiraling steel
ten maybe fifteen slippery feet
to the top where maybe
we could both stand
if we held on to each other
wary stylites or angels on a pinhead
tottering as we threw off
our clothes like heavy sails
the day propellers
made them obsolete
The warmth of your lips the chill
of steel rushing straight
up my back knowing there's
so much more of you to know
another language those silences
that always leave me offshore
reaching for more of you the way
what little Latin I know
or French or Italian or Spanish
so often leaves me wistful
stranded in a beautiful translation
that has an ocean of summer weather
and uncertainty at its fingertips
that leaves me a stranger
to myself among strangers

aboard HMS *Dubiety* again
with her whole blithering polyglot crew
fallen dumb and yearning
desperate for the music of a breeze
even if it sounds like it's scraped
off the bottom of a barrel
When overwhelmed by absence
their very being is reduced
to a wide-open listening
When words fail them
when sailing dim regions
and yellower climes
they find exactly
what is inscribed
on their limp yellow maps
Not what the words stand for
but the words themselves
spelled out in league-long letters
afloat on the milky sea
Slack-jawed hunched over the gunwales
they read in that sour daylight
Here the Darkness Begins Maybe
It takes days to drift clear
of each admonition
Beyond Maybe No Man Should Dare
Maybe days before yet another
slides off the stern
Here Doubt Sinks Maybe Deeper Than Prayer
So whittling figurines down
to a pile of shavings
sipping water out of tin cups
picking worms out of biscuits
they sprawl on deck
hopeless and clogged

when according to my calculations
maybe someone like me
someone who can't play a hunch
can take this wordless expanse
and calmly divide it by the way
you can sigh like distance
and swipe a breeze
out of a hollow sky
then maybe multiply that
by what it's like to listen to you
when you look down
and with a momentary
almost undetectable
night-soft flutter close your eyes
saying not yes not no not maybe

coda

Now on this cool narrow lake
your absence at evening
below the immeasurable in-between of twilight
I lie in parentheses
amused by how I can trace
in the glistening lines of this canoe
such a dear part of you
and between night and day
sweep up an armful of immediate odes
imagining I can lay them
before you and say
Here sift through these in the nibbling dark
There are more too many
for me to follow as they drip
off the dwindling light
or rise as the ridge darkens above pale water
the first house lights begin to appear
below the low dark hills
and the willows lean farther over the shore
Lines threaded by swallows and bats
that turn and dart every which way
skitter and slide
in and out of sight
and just when I think they're finished
they take off renewed by another ending
under opening and closing skies
inseparable beginning and end
as boundless as we wish to be
To listen and look at you
and press my face into your hair
a clear and happy senselessness

as a few weeks ago standing
on the dock watching fireworks
I didn't know where to look
and it didn't matter as they soared
the arc and sigh of fading rocketry
or their reflections the soft burst
and then the slow trail of lights
settling like starfire in black water
a surface I know as well as a blank page
as full and soft as twilight
when I can think of nothing more
to tell you then hear a sound
I never heard before
of maybe kingbirds
How they thrive above the cool water
click and snap in a whirl of dark sparks
so many of them their beaks clicking
as they swerve and dip in midair
stop and pluck whatever they want
wherever they may be

· *The Curious Builder* ·

The Curious Builder

A dream in which a butterfly crashes
through a stone wall is a warning
that you are no longer immune to flattery.

To dream that you are asleep means you will
soon receive gifts from people you detest.

To be told you often cackle loudly when asleep
means you are not a Master of Indifference.

A dream of rotten cactus signifies
that you have somehow offended the dead.

To receive an invitation in a dream
is the mark of an intelligent dreamer.

Short dreams are the dear price of a hectic life,
long dreams no compensation for a dull one.

To dream you are taller than usual
indicates that you are not very healthy
and may soon be attacked.

Following a dream in which someone empties
his pipe by tapping it against your forehead,
leave your bed and run, flee your house,
your village, never to return again.

Any dream that is a foe of sympathy
is no friend of magic.

When a dream's music is sweet,
give all you own to the poor;
when it is harsh, leave all you own
on the doorsteps of the rich.
Then, in either case, you must flee
your home, your village,
never to return again.

A dream of lambs bounding over rainbows:
this is where the songs of fiends arise.

Even to Artemidorus, a dream
of eating uncooked corn
does not easily reveal its secret.

If you dream your house is full
of jovial foreigners, imperturbable,
look-alike heathens
who speak an incomprehensible tongue
and who refuse to leave
no matter how many gifts you throw at them,
then when you wake
know that there will be beauty
all around you, peace within your heart
—before you must quietly depart,
forsaking your house, your village,
never to return again.

But if dreaming your way
through your own house,
or any familiar place, you open
a cabinet or door
that you, somehow, never noticed before,

and enter a room or a corridor
that leads to another,
and yet another,

and you find yourself
not in a parlous maze
but a maze of openings, exploring
an expanding mansion
that must have been there all along,
then you should welcome these dreams
as their blooming enjambment
welcomes you, and like a bank president
who takes a look around one morning
and declares: "Let's convert this place
into a restaurant!"—you can expect
one of your better days.

After such dreams, whether
he wants to or not,
a man prospers, reassured
that even in the reign of Bogus I,
enough pleasure and worth remain
for someone to finally slide
into bed again
with gratitude waiting behind closed eyes
like starlight reflected in black ice.

Or, if his heart be overfull
and repose impossible,
if his head still throngs
with all he profited yet still craves,
he must forget about sleep
and dreams, but rise again
and declare:

I, Paul Violi, being of sound mind
—Say, the sound of skidmarks
formed where the view across the Hudson
suddenly offers the faces
of Frank Lloyd Wright,
D.W. Griffith, Ezra Pound,
and Buster Keaton
carved in the Palisades.

Or the skidmarks themselves,
as much astonishment's own shadow
as Icho's brushstroke,
lead the way back to Manhattan
through Suburbia and the footfalls
of Tyrannosaurus Bronx.

There, along wasted shoreline
and burned-out piers,
Curiosity—what The Worthies
called "Desire's fingertips"—
finds a way out
of another wreck—tangles
of melted steel, red rust,
stumps, and slow water—
in time to conduct
the chain-link music of concertina wire
and shredded plastic in a freezing wind,
and set the dome of evening
on rooftop corners
squinched with dirt and sand.

Like water, almost knowing
where it's going, it leads
along a maze of downtown streets
until under the absolute beauty
of the dark blue night

you must stop and declare:
—Who? Me? No, I was just looking
for this restaurant.
It's around here somewhere.

It used to be a bank
and it smells like a basement,
a dungeon in bloom.
Uneven plank-and-slab flooring,
cinemascope windows,
sky-washed marble-plated walls,

one vast dim room
that brightened as it rose
to a tiled ceiling spanned
by iron beams painted silver:
the kind of place where Mary Magdalene
first laid eyes on
"Blinkers" the Phoenician.

It's on a corner.
I've been there before,
two or three evenings,
and each time it had changed,
expanded into another room
furnished the same haphazard way:
jammed with mismatched tables
and chairs, storage-room couches,
faded carpets and crimson drapes,
wormwood and brass,
blue willow bowls
arrayed behind the mahogany bar,
griffins and grape vines
carved in gold-frame mirrors
hung too high to reflect anybody,

and waiters who have to swat
away the plants to find you.
A gang of waiters
so insultingly polite
Have A Nice Day
is tattooed on their tongues.

"Today's special, Phoenix Wing,
might be a bit over your head, Sir.

"Need I explain the potluck
Thyestean Menu, Sir?

"The turtle never stops growing
until the day it dies.
Unlike some of us . . . eh, Sir?

"Or, perhaps to do justice
to your favorite metrical foot,
the Pterodactyl?

"Might you care for bread, cold meat,
fruit, and a porridge of spelt?
Or something not so frugal?"

No, I'll try the peacock from Samos,
hazel hens from Phrygia, and . . .
cranes from Medea, kid from Abracia,
tunnyfish from Chalcedon,
lampreys from Tartessus, whitefish
from Pessinus, swordfish from Rhodes,
oysters from Tarentum, scallops
from Chios, parrot fish from Cilicia,
and throw in some nuts from Thásos,
dates from Egypt, and, yes,
acorns from Iberia.

. . . There goes the waitress
with the streambed eyes . . .

Every order served
on commemorative plates
honoring the orotund and congenial:
Rabelais, Samuel Daniel,
The Wife of Bath, Aretino;
Eleanor of Aquitaine, Falstaff,
Coleridge, Gibbon, Orson Welles,
Catherine de' Medici, Mama Cass.

Every table a hive of conversation,
except the nearest, where
amid contending anecdotes, one diner
declares: "You think *that's* disgusting?
Listen to this!"

One night, after months
in a northwestern province,
I'm staring up through the mosquito net
hung high, slung low from the poles.
It forms a sort of tent
within a tent . . .

browns and greens, light and dark,
cavernous folds, all peaks
and droops and dim exaggerations
where my last waking moment
flies off like a weary bat
in a cathedral.

It's merely the fever coming back,
dengue, seeping through me, cold
and empty and strange.

I shiver in the sagging cot,
snuff a candle, squash a cigarette
in a bottlecap ashtray,
and fall asleep.

But for how long I don't know
before the nausea hits,
wakes me on the lunge,
hauls me to the side, where
face pressed into the netting,
I start to heave, too weak to care.
—Some enormous creature I was,
stuck in a tar pit, mind
awhirl like a crippled fly.

The next time I wake up
I feel fine, oblivious
to what happened,
except I can't open my eyes.
The lids are stuck, glued shut.
Cheeks stiff, nose clogged,
it's me, with the netting
pasted over my face—Smithereens' clown.

The joke's on me.
I peel it off, gently, like a mask.
And as convincing as, say,
The Shroud of Turin,
the image snared in the threads
—Gimme an H! Gimme a U!
Gimme an M, Gimme an I, Gimme an L!
Gimme another I! and a T and a Y!
Waddaya get?

—Who? Me? I don't get it.
The only thing The Shroud of Turin
reminds me of is the tablecloths
in this place.
Every dream, every journey
is a digression, but from what
I don't know: Dreaming or not,
on our better days we're tracing
the same immanent pattern of fascination.
The other night, for example,

I'm coasting down these long halls,
entranced by commonplace things;
I run my fingertips along threads
of silver and gold in the walls,
casually asking
which is memory, which desire.
Then, opening a side door
I happen to notice, I enter
and there it is:

Vast, hollow, Everestian heights.
There it is: Loss.
A lurid, pendulous light,
stale gold fumes draped
above an ocean of dust, silt
so fine a raindrop would float on it.
A wonder of annihilation
or an annihilated wonder.

And in the far distance
two wandering figures appear,
dressed not like explorers
but plodding tourists
who have found hell a disappointment
and want a refund,

who have no sense
of what has been lost,
but still think the bus
must be around here someplace.

A mile away from me in the dunes
and yet I can hear one of them declare:
"Would you believe it,
that even Nothingness
could be so full of itself?"

I'm still trying to figure
that one out days later
when I walk in here and see
in the pargeting above the door
a line from Fitzgerald's *Odyssey:*
"Charmed out of time, we see
no life can be hid from our dreaming."

I almost have that one figured out
when I hear an imperial fingersnap
and I'm greeted
by The Waiters' Serenade:

"Chew on ice, eat a smile.
    Chew on smoke, dream awhile.
        (Sing it Jimmy Boy,
    Sing it for the hoi polloi.)

Chew on ice, let it fade . . .
    Chew on smoke . . . the life you made."

I almost figure that one out
when—another fingersnap—

I'm led through a maze
of continuous renovation,
tables and scaffolds and workers,
and I'm seated just in time
below a great old mirror
flaked with black rot
where a long-sought image
of all I've loved and made
and hope to keep
is about to finally burn through silver
and drop right into my plate.

Of course there is a slight wait,
during which I order a cocktail
or two, watch the construction,
offer some advice, grow impatient,
skim a magazine, write a few letters,
send them off, skim a novel,
and am about to complain
when the waitress arrives,
apologizes for the confusion,
and delivers my mail.

Dear Reader,
     Since the reign of Bogus I

Dear Wordsmith,
     We are off to hunt truth and rabbits,
so saddle your ox!
     We'll take the shortcut again,
through swamp and paradox

To Whom It May Concern,
     It is with great regret
that we inform you

Dear Chump,
   You will undoubtedly want to be there
when Gullibility and Greed renew their vows

Beloved Patron,
   It is with a heavy head and
shriven heart that I take pen in hand

Dear Applicant,
   The subject may appear remote at first,
but Creative Freedom versus Social
Responsibility is the question we wish
to explore with you today

Dear Parent,
   Was it mere pedantry to reject those
ransom notes for your loved ones
because of the grammatical errors
they contained or were higher principles

Dear Investor,
   By the time you read this letter
I will be gone. I have run away.
My plan to invest your savings
in the manufacture of styrofoam coffins
was, I admit, a sham; and the implant
that would allow the common man
to convert his big toenail
into a television screen

Dear Finalist,
   Due to an error that we expect you
to find as difficult to understand as
it is for us to explain, our previous
notification designating you as a winner

Dear Subscriber,
    In the latest edition
of *The Illustrated Dictionary*
under the entry for "nonplus,"
an old coot frantically sweeps
a pile of dust across a trackless desert
right up to your feet
and without stopping, without
even looking up at you, declares:
"Out of my way, you desperate bastard!"
    Now for only a few dollars a month
this and many more memorable

Say Hey, Peewee!
    Forswore hoity-toity melee?
Bandstand hubbub so-so?
Zoot suit heyday undone?
Juju hodgepodge humdrum?
Eenie-meanie payday? Holus-bolus shit-fit?
    If this be the case, then we
strongly recommend Mayday! Mayday!
Backtrack: Waylay Lulu, murmur Tufu,
kowtow paxwax booboo,
maintain bedspread handstand

Dear Contestant,
    Congratulations! Your chance to win
the dreamhouse of a lifetime, to live
on the edge of rampant transformation
is at your fingertips.
    Just pick up your pen

Dearest Occupant,
    This building has been condemned STOP

Your constant delays leave us no
alternative STOP Vital services will be
terminated STOP To facilitate your
immediate departure we advise you
to avail yourself of the next

To The Reader,

Behold once more with serious labor here
Have I refurnished out this little frame,
Repaired some parts defective here and there,
And passages new added to the same,
Some rooms enlarged, made some less than they were
Like to the curious builder who this year
Pulls down, and alters what he did the last
As if the thing in doing were more dear
Than being done, and nothing likes that's past.
        For that we ever make the latter day
The scholar of the former, and we find
Something is still amiss that must delay
Our business, and leave work for us behind.
As if there were no Sabbath of the mind.
And howsoever be it well or ill
What I have done, it is mine own I may
Do whatsoever therewithall I will.
        I may pull down, raise, and re-edify
It is the building of my life the fee
Of Nature, all the inheritance that I
Shall leave to those which must come after me
And all the care I have is but to see
These lodgings of my affections neatly drest
Wherein so many noble friends there be
Whose memories with mine must therein rest.

from
· The Hazards of Imagery ·

"The frescoes in the castle are by
Pisano, and they are so smooth and
shining that even today you can see
your own reflection in them."
　　　　　　　　　—The Anonimo

In The House of Messer Sconforto

In the solarium can be found
a famous representation
of giants in chiaroscuro,
singing and dancing
and tromping about the earth.
It is called Hymn to the Obvious.
It is a mysterious work,
an audible darkness,
and it is unforgivable.

In the sanctuary, to the right,
is an oil painting in which
Vitality is represented, wide-eyed
at the moment of waking, saluting
Death in the form of a toad
sitting on his belly.
It is an early example
of that type of brushwork
in which each stroke
is called a snarl.
Nevertheless, it, too,
is an unforgivable work,
scruffy and audacious,
cheerless and fireproof.

In the music room two busts
serve as a pair of bookends.
One portrays the young king
Mithradates,
who to make himself invulnerable
to assassins, sampled
poison every day; the other,

the old Mithradates,
who when he desired to end
his life, could not find
a poison strong enough to do the job.
They are carved in stone.
Very hard stone.
But not that hard.

In the dining hall the group portrait
of a family weeping as they stand
over a puddle of milk
is by an unknown hand.
Many presume it is waterproof.
In fact, the application
of the slightest pressure reveals
it is painted on an enormous sponge
that has recently been dunked.

In the mezzanine, Sprezzante
has painted The Great Cramp.
Is it eternity, you ask, running
your fingertips across the cool wall,
or the loss of it?
Facing it is his masterpiece: The Shrug.

At The Chapel Cardinal Finale

Here is a painting on wood
by an unknown hand,
of hearty fishermen in an open boat,
hauling a cow out of the Bay of Naples.
This painting smells:
an unfortunate odor no one
can eradicate or name.

Here, too, is a painting of the savior
from whose eyes many have attested
they have seen real tears fall.
And I for one believe it to be so.
For I have heard this said
of other paintings
and recalling how they are all
so unbelievably bad,
so poorly executed,
I have concluded that it is
the painters' utter ineptitude
that has made their very subject weep.
Such is the miraculous power of art.

At The Tomb of The
Improperly Trained Bombardiers

This is the saddest work I have ever seen.
A tremendous concrete piano,
its maker unknown, yet
—O soul of man! unutterable sorrow!
Impenetrable silence!
The Great Echo!

The poems framed in the corridor
are by Maginot.
They are thick, the lines
impenetrable, true vers Maginot,
and visitors are advised
to simply go around them.

In The Gift Shop at The Lunatic Asylum

Always on sale, the figurines
of infants are made out of tar
and are produced by inmates,
former apprentices
of Imbrolgione mostly.
On visiting days family
and friends purchase them
as presents for the inmates.

Here, too, Junior Achievers
can always join
the Aesthetics Club
and the Restoration Committee tours
that begin and end with the murals
of Mad Emmett, who even when
confined, isolated, deprived
of brush and palette,
continued to pursue
the beautiful, the ideal,
by painting the walls of his cell
with his own—his own—with his—
I dare not say what!

In The Banco Grosso

Like many Romans
the ingenious Sprezzante,
the same who conceived
and designed the tollbooths
on the Via Dolorosa,
believed a tribute should display
the glory of the subject
without correcting his imperfections
or attempting to conceal them
from the eyes of the world.
Among his works here
is the snazzy lifelike figure
of the surgeon Gianfrio,
who preferred to operate in the nude.
So tightly has the canvas
been stretched that the indignant,
the embittered, the vengeful,
are often re-injured
by the rebounding objects
they throw at it, and have to be
taken back to the hospital.

In The Lounge at The Physicians' Guild

The standing nudes and odalisques
are by Pale Otis, The Swooner;
and his model was his beloved.
With her before him, at times
in a nightgown so sheer
she looked like a lily
afloat in a crystal vase,
he perfected that style
in which her limbs,
her munificent thighs,
are never outlined
but fluttered and rubbed,
gradations of light and dark
caressed to the drowsy transparency
of a pink flower
beneath the wings of a honeybee,
or a shoreline at high noon
to a wayworn sailor's eye.
He himself called it "strumming,"
drawing a plucked string,
the sweetest, most languid string
of the lute the moment before
it comes to rest, to show
how the sight of her
erased the line
between reason and rapture.

And he took care to preserve
these drawings with a fixative,
smudge-proof and fast-drying,

that did not alter his technique
or the texture of the paper;
that dried in seconds and caused
the least possible change
to delicate tints and values.

And he always tried to follow
directions, holding the can
at a 45 degree angle
12 – 14 inches above the drawing,
starting at the bottom, spraying
from side to side in overlapping
strokes as he proceeded to the top.

And this fixative contained ethanol,
methanol, and ethyl acetate.
And when he got some in his eyes
his assistants had to flush them
with water for fifteen minutes
and call for a noteworthy physician.
And when he inhaled it
his trusty assistants
would comfort his beloved
and call for a noteworthy physician
who would treat him
for injury to his blood
and kidneys and lungs.
And when he ingested it
he suffered confusion and headache,
instability and paralysis.
And to induce vomiting
his assistants would drag him
out into the yard and throw him
over the back of a mule,

then play cards in the shade
with his beloved and console her
until a noteworthy physician arrived
and a paler Otis was fully revived.

At The Tavern of Messer Angelo
on Via Canale

The colossal nudes, Hercules
and Voluptuousness on a seesaw;
the mezzo-relievo of youths
who have wreathed their heads
in roses to cool their brains
while drinking wine;
the figures of the Queen
of the Goths bouncing
the God of Apology off a tree:
these are all antique.

On a large canvas in the hallway
is an altogether remarkable work:
Venus reclines in the golden arms
of common day, her eyelids a bit weary,
her glowing thighs as slick as wet clay.

Various silk tapestries
hang free from the rafters,
the work of an artist
who kept his eyes not solely
on man working in the dust,
nor on gods dreaming clouds on high,
but on the glowing rains
that hold them for an hour or so
in each other's thoughts.

One portrays Hermes, the glad god,
who moved faster than luck

or thought; who stole
what he could not himself create;
who first made music
—made it so effortlessly he seemed
to swipe it from the air—
and the first song he chose to sing
was a celebration of his own begetting.
(Trustworthy people have told me
that this work was filched
from the Tomb of the Secretary of Labor.)

Another, above the couch,
is said to represent
the devoted Lodovico, considering
the whorls of his lady's thumbprint
as a topographical map
of Mount Parnassus.

With the painting that shows Cupid
gazing into a mirror
that does not reflect his image,
Gaspari the Syrian poses
the question: When love can appear
so swiftly as to sneak up
on a mirror, how can mortals
and most gods defend themselves
against such a force?

The mailbox, painted dark blue,
sits atop a tilted cedar post.
It has a little red flag on one side
and it is altogether remarkable.

The Toyota in the driveway
is very old and is said
to have come from Japan.

There is in the hallway
an immense dogfood bowl.
It is made of iridescent pink plastic.
It is, as I have said, immense
and it is hideous.

In the kitchenette is a statuette
of Ceres, Goddess of Wheaties.

The dishwasher is a Kenmore
and altogether worthy of praise.

In the foyer the oversized painting
of a pork chop provides
visitors many opportunities
for conversation.

In the servants' quarters
there are many impressive works
that stress the imminence of death
and the probability of hell fire.

Placed on the broad maplewood table
beside bottles of cognac
there is a recording device
with a silver megaphone
into which natives are often
invited to shout
the oral histories of their people.

We whose hearts have been gripped
by life, scoff at the idea of art
as mere ornamentation: So they
seem to proclaim,
the three statues that adorn
the neighbor's lawn, plaster deer
with real bulletholes in them.

Notes

Harmatan

I arrived in Nigeria during December, 1966, and left in June, 1967.

Hausa, Ibo, Yoruba, Tuareg, Fulani, and Tiv are the names of the tribes. Lugard (Sir Frederick Lugard) was British Royal High Commissioner of Northern Nigeria in the early 1900s. Ex-pat is an abbreviation for ex-patriate, usually a European working for the Nigerian government. Bature means learned European gentleman, but, depending on the inflection, can also mean something considerably less complimentary. Exactly what, I forget. A High Life Club is where people dance the High Life to High Life music. Star Beer tastes better than Coors, Three Rings taste like stale Lucky Strikes. St. Augustine said (somewhere): "And I entered the fields and wide palaces of memory."

King Nasty

A few phrases and observations in this poem are from Carlyle's *French Revolution Vol. III* and *Characters and Commentaries* by Lytton Strachey. The anecdote concerning the pirate Stoertebeker can be found in *Folklore and the Sea*, by Beck, Wesleyen U. Press.

Wet Bread and Roasted Pearls

The numbers in this poem follow ascending and descending Fibonacci progressions that intersect on the image of a sunset reflected in a flooded field.

The Curious Builder

The conclusion of the poem is taken from the opening lines of Samuel Daniel's poem "To the Reader."

The Hazards of Imagery

The introductory quotation is from George C. Williamson's edition of the *Anonimo* translated by Palolo Mussi. A 16th century catalogue used by historians to identify various art works around the Veneto, its author's identity remains obscure. Hence, the eponymous anonymous.